MIX-TAPE

How to Stop Listening to the Recordings of Your Past

KATE GARNES

MIX-TAPE

How to Stop Listening to
the Recordings of Your Past

CONTENTS: THE RECORDINGS

For my dad,
who left too soon.

Thank you for the story.

INTRODUCTION

I'd like for you to imagine the moment right before you do something scary. Choose carefully, because I want it to be something so terrifying that it makes you sick to your stomach. I mean, not just sick to your stomach, but also nervous and excited and terrified all at the same time.

Skydiving.

Asking someone out on a date.

Buying a car.

Riding the *Tower of Terror* at Disney World. (I'll have to take your word for that one, because I do subject myself to that particular fear. I do not do drops.)

Or how about the moment before you tell someone a very personal story about your very personal life. A story you haven't told. A story that is scary to tell.

Welcome to my reality right now.

That nervous-excited-terrified stomachache... it's happening inside me right this minute.

The idea of writing my story is terrifying. Putting my story out to the world? *Gulp.*

So why am I doing this? Maybe that's the question you're asking... it's certainly the question *I* am asking.

Well, it's the first question. It's followed shortly by a louder, more important question: What if someone needs to hear my story?

What if *you* need to hear it? Maybe you need to know the songs that have composed the mixtape of my life.

So, my friend, let's do this.

My name is Kate Garnes, and I'd like to tell you my story.

Let's start with something easy for me to talk about, something I suspect we can all relate to: the power of music.

Music can change you. Music can shape you. One song can change your life.

One song can save you. Another song can break you to your core.

One verse can give you hope. One phrase can give you peace.

Music is what I grew up with, and my mom once told me that I was singing myself to sleep before I could talk. You guys, *I love music.*

A few decades ago, DJs coined the term *mixtape* to describe a collection of songs from various artists, each carefully chosen, mixed, and recorded into a group of their own. Today, we call it a playlist on your phone, and it's the same idea. This collection of songs was chosen because they fall into a category that makes sense to you.

Here is what I want you to know: I have lived my whole life inside the loop of one crazy mixtape. I don't mean just songs. I mean words. Voices. Comments. Criticisms. Ever since I was a kid, I have had played repeated sound bytes in my head, the voices of others telling me I am not good enough, not pretty enough, not smart enough.

Have you ever had a song stuck in your head? What happens when it's a voice? A voice you'd like to forget?

Everyone has that one song that plays over and over. You may have had a recording in your head that has held you down. You've tried to change the song, but somehow that recording ends up on repeat, no matter how you try to silence it. We have lots of voices competing for our attention, and I am here to help you choose the right ones.

Right now, you're holding my story, my recording, my mixtape.

My mission, sweet friend, is to help you silence that recording you've had playing on repeat. Someone has told you you're not good enough, or maybe they've said you're too much. They've said you're too fat or too thin, too manly or too girly. Too short or too tall. Too whatever else.

With some careful crafting, choosing, and recording, we get to change the mixtape. And starting here, I am going to take you through my journey of remixing those

3

ugly recordings into words and songs of truth, growth, and bad-assery.

I am not going to sugarcoat it, so let's be real: changing your recordings is hard work. If it were easy, everyone would do it, and we wouldn't have this problem in the first place. It's not easy, but it's worth it. And I suspect you're here because you're ready for change.

Stick with me, even when it's hard to hear what I am saying. I'll honor your story as I share mine, and I'll help you become the DJ of your own life. Create your own mixtape.

Let's do this.

CHAPTER 1

THE RECORDING: "I AM NOT WORTH SHOWING UP FOR"

I am not a stranger to the dark.
Hide away, they say, 'cause we don't want your broken parts...
I've learned to be ashamed of all my scars.
Run away, they say, no one will love you as you are.

~ *"This is Me" from The Greatest Showman*

~ ~ ~

Words have power.

Words are heavy with meaning, intended or not.

It doesn't take much, and it doesn't take long. One comment. One song. One moment.

One comment from someone can cut you to your core, while another comment can transport you from utter despair to exceeding joy.

Think with me. Close your eyes and recall a time when someone said something that changed you. Think of their words and consider how they affected the way you viewed yourself.

Think carefully. I'll wait for you.

Do you have it? Not yet?

Give yourself more time. Think harder.

We each have these recordings that play on a loop in our minds.

Let yours emerge.

While you're thinking, I'll tell you mine.

As the only child in my Missouri home, I grew up with a vivid imagination. One day, I was a blacksmith in the early settler days of the Wild West. I took telephone orders for hooks and metal doorknobs, and then I "shipped them to my customers" all around the world. Another day, I was a pirate on a ship sailing to the New World from the treehouse in my backyard. Often, I became a world class singer. I watched videos of Britany Spears or Celine Dion, and I would imagine myself standing on stage next to them, belting out their greatest hits.

I became what I imagined, and most of the time, I imagined I was a detective. That was my favorite pastime of all. This was around 1996, when the movie *Harriet the Spy* came out. Now, I don't mean to brag, but I think it's safe to say that I was the best detective in all the Midwest. I was a pro at hiding in bushes, making observations, and taking copious notes. I took notes about babies crying, doors shutting, or—my favorite offender—my neighbor Ted, who listened to NPR or Garth Brooks on repeat while cleaning his garage. My pink and blue bathrobe became a very stylish trench coat that every good detective must wear. (Clearly, I was not hurting for an imagination.)

Every detective knows how to be sly, and I was one stealthy ninja. I could slither into the kitchen, get a fruit roll-up, and return to my lair without being spotted by my mom or even by my cat Tiger. And I was an expert at tapping into phone conversations. I might even say that was my winning accomplishment. I am sure you know that all the bad guys speak in code on the phone, and it was the job of Kate the Spy to decipher the puzzle.

I was deeply immersed into a top-secret case when I snuck into my closet with the phone. I did the whole trick the experts use. Just in case you have an old-fashioned rotary phone, you'll want to know this trick for expert eavesdropping: 1) Pick up the receiver, but keep your finger on the hook so nobody hears you pick it up right away. 2) Hold the phone close to your ear, then so carefully and gently lift your finger from the hook, thereby silently jumping head-first into the secret conversation. Technically, it's illegal, but telephone laws weren't my top concern two decades ago.

Holding my breath, I listened. I knew that Agent Mom was trying to get answers out of the bad guy on the other side, and I wanted the scoop.

"What is your problem, Judi?"

"Jack, you didn't even show up to hear her sing her first solo at church. You hurt her feelings," Agent Mom said.

9

I heard a man's voice say, "Well, she's no Mariah Carey."

Silence on the phone line.

I knew that voice, I thought... and then I gasped with recognition, immediately putting my hand over my mouth. I had made the fatal error of tapping into phone calls: I let them hear me.

"Kate?" My dad said my name.

But he didn't say it like normal. Not like your basic, simple, easy-to-say *Kate.* No, it sounded like *cayT.* A very hard, over-pronounced *T.*

Whenever the T was over-pronounced, I knew I was in some serious. Like, hide-under-the-bed kind of trouble.

I hung up the phone.

The game was over. I was no longer a detective. I was a seven-year-old girl who had just heard her father say she wasn't good enough.

What I didn't understand yet were the effects of alcohol. I didn't know that my dad had had too much to drink, and I didn't know how a person changes when they are drunk. I only knew my dad had spoken words that must be true. I wasn't a good singer, and I wasn't worthy of his presence. If I had a solo, it wasn't good enough for him to show up and listen.

I hid in my closet for what seemed like an hour, which in seven-year-old terms was probably more like five minutes. Since every good detective has a mirror and a flashlight in her pocket at all times, I grabbed both and practiced making funny faces at my reflection. After all, a good detective doesn't show when she is sad. A great detective never cries at all. All the best detectives can laugh, even when they are sad.

So, I laughed.

I scrunched my eyebrows, nose, and mouth into every funny face I could think of in my hand-held mirror, all to trick myself, to make my tears seem like tears of joy. I stuck my tongue out, pushed my eyebrows together, and puffed my cheeks up like a blowfish. I covered my sadness and insecurity with masks of laughter and joy. Nobody looks sad when they are laughing. So, I laughed.

The fact is, in that moment, I was no longer a detective.

I was a girl who had just heard her father speak a recording that would stay with her as long as she has breath.

I learned that I was not a good enough singer.

I learned that I was not a good enough daughter.

I learned that I was not good enough.

Not good enough for my dad.

Not good enough for anyone.

And yet, on that day as I hid in the closet, wearing my pink and blue bathrobe, I vowed that I would never let anyone see that I knew the truth. I had learned the secret that I wasn't good enough, but I would never let them know.

If I was sad, I would laugh.

If I was angry, I would laugh.

When someone jumped out from behind a doorway and scared me so much that I peed a little, I would laugh.

When my cat Tiger passed away after giving me so many years of kitty snuggles, I laughed to hide the pain.

When I felt anything at all, I laughed. Laughter was a mask, and I wore it always.

And so, now you know my first recording: I am not good enough.

Before that day, I had only ever really wanted to be a singer. Sure, I pretended to be lots of things, but even with all of my imagining, my daydreams paled in the light of myself on the stage. I wanted to sing, and I would have told you so. I was going to be a singer! I loved singing!

Failure was not an option, and I am not even sure I knew what failure meant. But if my dad said I wasn't good at it, he must be right. After all, he was my dad. He was the man of my life. He was supposed to be my protector. He was the one who was supposed to show me unconditional love and trust.

I mean, that's what parents are for right? To show us true sacrificial love and joy? To give us a tangible example of how to be a good person?

He was my dad. I trusted him, because that's what you're supposed to do. I was a good daughter. When he spoke, I listened, and I believed him. And I had heard him say I wasn't good enough.

From that day forward, I doubted myself. I doubted not only my ability to sing, but I doubted my abilities and worth in everything I did.

Isn't that sad? One overheard comment from a person I trusted made me let go of my dream.

As I said, it doesn't take much, and it doesn't take long. One comment. One song. One moment.

May you have some thoughts rolling around in your head right now. Maybe my story led you to recall that one comment. Maybe you're thinking of that person who told you that you were too fat to play on the swings on the playground. The parent who pushed you up against the wall because you got a B on your algebra test. The neighbor kid who outed you to your crush for being a "Jesus Freak" and knowing all of the words to the Veggie Tales song "Water Buffalo." The classmate who told you that you couldn't sit at their table because you weren't "black" enough. The grandma who pushed food in front of your face because if you didn't fatten up, you'd never find a husband.

You have a recording like mine, I am willing to bet. And I am also pretty sure you know the one I mean. One comment from one person completely shifted your outlook on yourself—and on life itself.

That comment matters, even if it hurts to remember it. That comment grew into a thought that became a truth, and whether you like it or not, it created you into who you are today.

It sucks, doesn't it? Mostly, it sucks because it wasn't your fault.

Let me say that one more time. Listen carefully. Ready?

It wasn't your fault.

I can say this to you with confidence, because I have needed to say it to me, too.

It wasn't my fault when a first grader named Joe decided to let everyone in his class know that I walked weird. I had passed him in the hallway, he noticed, and he told people. Too many people. He made kindergarten-me feel bad, and now thirty-year-old-me still changes out my tennis shoes more often than necessary because I don't want people to notice that I walk funny. (I had club feet when I was born, and that is also not my fault. But we will talk about that later.)

It wasn't Laura's fault when fifteen-year-old Bobby said she looked like the little girl dressed like a bumblebee on the cover of her favorite Smashing Pumpkins album. It wasn't her fault, but forty years later, Laura still reflexively changes the radio station anytime a song from that album plays in her car.

It wasn't Melanie's fault that she was raised by a dad who would not allow crying. If she or her siblings ever started to cry, her father responded, "You want to cry? I'll give you something to cry about." It wasn't her fault, but twenty-four-year-old Melanie still resorts to anger instead of tears when something upsets her. She believes that crying exposes weakness, and she has promised to never let anyone view her as weak. She refuses to cry even in front of her husband.

It wasn't Tara's fault that she was shunned from sitting with the other African American girls in the sixth grade, because they decided "she talked too much like a white girl." To this day, Tara still tries to make herself small, invisible, and to even appear uneducated around certain people. She doesn't want them to know that she's incredibly smart, and she wants to hide the secret that she has an extremely high IQ—all for fear of not being accepted by those who look like her.

It's not your fault that you have learned to wear any kind of mask to cover up the scars on your soul. Maybe you laugh to hide the searing pain in your chest when someone makes fun of your outfit. Maybe you get a tough, rugged exterior when someone calls you weak or soft, just so you can prove them wrong. Maybe you are longing for

15

someone to tell you it's okay to feel sad, or it's okay to not have all the answers. Maybe you puff out your chest and hurl insults at your friends because you're trying to hide the fact that you are terrified of not being good enough. Maybe you wear layers of masks, all to hopefully distract anyone from seeing the true pain that has been brewing from years of neglect and pain.

It's not your fault.
But it is your problem.

I grew up believing that recording in my head.
I grew up believing that I wasn't enough.
I believed I wasn't worth showing up for.
I believed I couldn't sing, dance, or become anything—not even a detective.

Today is a new day. Today, we are going to start taping over that recording.

Unfortunately, those lies will always be there. Sort of like the nineties song *MMMBop* by Hanson, it won't ever fully go away. Your recording has become a part of you.

But I have good news. In these chapters together, I can teach you how to change the melody of that recording. Together, we will find a song that speaks truth to you.

It will speak the truths you should have been listening to all along.

It's not your fault, but I am about to help you solve your problem.

Buckle up, friend. It's showtime.

Remix

Can you think of a time when someone's words or opinions became your truth?

What did they say?

How did you hear it?

How did you handle it?

How do those words still affect you today?

CHAPTER 2

THE RECORDING: "I CAN'T KEEP UP"

She dreams she's dancing...
around and around, without any cares."

~ *"Sarah Beth" by Rascal Flatts*

~ ~ ~

Dance.

It's a polarizing word.

For some people, the word *dance* brings anxiety and fear from the anxious memories of stepping onto a dance floor and making a fool of themselves with their lack of rhythm. They feel far more comfortable watching their friends dance from the safety of a chair in the corner.

For others, the word *dance* literally means *dancing like nobody is watching*, because that's the only time they feel confident to even remotely let loose. They're only going to cut a rug under careful conditions: if they are alone, wearing their comfy pajama pants, eating ice cream, and listening to *Living on A Prayer* for the fiftieth time.

Some hear the word *dance*, and they visualize a huge stage, pointe ballet shoes, and countless hours in training with blood, sweat, and tears. These same people also envision standing ovations from audiences wearing designer gowns and opera glasses.

Someone else may think of hip-hop dancers in the streets of New York, where suddenly every driver, construction worker, and homeless man becomes a drummer while they tap dance or "Pop and Lock" their way down 5th Avenue.

To some, the word *dance* is *freedom*. The word evokes invitations to go out with your friends and live your best life with anyone and everyone who will join you on the dance floor. It doesn't matter if you're rocking the Carlton, hitting a Fortnight dance, or busting out the Charleston. You hear the music, and your body starts to move.

To me, *dance* means beauty and grace. Dancing was freedom for me. It felt like a cool breath of fresh air, or the feeling of waking up on Christmas morning. Imagine true happiness. That was dance to me.

There was just one problem. I do not have the feet of a dancer.

They weren't even the feet of someone who could walk easily.

I was born with club feet.

Now, if you are like most people, you probably have zero idea what I am talking about, and that's fair. I wish I could tell you that club feet were made to party, that I have superhuman powers to be the best dancer in any night club. I assure you, if that were true, I would have gone out a whole lot more. While that's an amazing dream, it was not the case.

Super smart doctors call my condition Talipes Valgus, and it basically means that my feet were twisted and turned in at birth. As a newborn, my tiny legs and feet curved like the letter J. The bones were twisted so that the bottoms of my feet faced each other. Left untreated, I would have struggled to walk at all.

Now, keep in mind, I was born back in 1988. (Yes, I know this reveals my age, but worse things could be discovered about me, like the fact that I prefer unsweetened tea over sweet tea, or that I am a terrible sleep talker.) Anyway, in 1988, nobody had smartphones or Netflix. We didn't have WebMD—or even Google, for that matter—to look up needless information. I mean, it wasn't the Stone Age; we did have microwaves, Barbies, Disney movies, Hamburger Helper, and the beginnings of MTV. But the medical world had a long way to go. A diagnosis of club feet was not yet their specialty.

When the doctors first saw my feet, they put metal braces on both legs. I was strapped into those contraptions for the first ten months of my life. If I had been born in 2019, they probably would been crafted into some amazing color, equipped with their own smart capabilities to play music and teach me a second language. Alas, they were plain gray with no Wi-Fi capabilities. After ten months, it was clear that the braces weren't going to cut it, and surgery was the only answer.

When I was less than a year old, I had major surgery to correct both of my feet. The doctors told my mom that the tendons near my toes were the width of a human hair. This explains why I have one toe that I physically can't move, since they nicked that teeny-tiny tendon during surgery.

My surgeon told my mom that a few things would be true: I would always walk funny; I would have poor motor skills in my feet and legs; and I wouldn't be able to physically keep up with other kids my age. They drew these conclusions before my first birthday.

Did you catch the timing of that? Before I could even understand the words *feet, surgeon,* or *walk funny,* someone spoke weaknesses and downfalls into my existence.

While I focused on figuring out how to be a person, how to know when I needed to eat, sleep, and poop, people spoke limitations over me. I couldn't stand up for myself. (In fact, I couldn't stand up at all.) I had no control over the decisions, diagnoses, and labels applied to my life.

That sucks, right?

Maybe you can relate.

Perhaps someone has spoken untruths about you or your abilities. Maybe when they met you, they decided that they know who you are. Unfortunately, we do have the human tendency to make snap judgements about people. But snap judgements lead to snap opinions, which lead to snap comments.

We can't control the words that other people speak about us, and that is a painful reality. But we can control whether we allow those words to limit us or to hinder our view of who we are.

Let's jump back to the top: dancing. Dance was one skill the doctors decided that I would never excel in. The thing is, nobody told me that. At least not then. And I am thankful for that lucky mistake on their part.

My mom started me in gymnastics before we tried dance, and it wasn't a win for me. Now, hear me out, gymnasts of the world. All the other tiny humans were smiling and jumping on the trampolines, running across the floor mats, doing cartwheels that resembled a bear crawl, and swinging like a monkey on the uneven bars. Not little Kate. The balance beam was my arch nemesis. I still contend that there is a special place in H-E-double-hockey-sticks for whomever had the sick and twisted idea to create a beam three feet off the ground for a little girl in a tiny 2-foot, 7-inch frame. There was zero chance I was going to attempt to walk across that death trap, and my screams and sobs let everybody in the gym know it.

So, dance class it was.

I started off in a ballet and tap combo class for baby dancers, and I found my calling. I discovered my passion. *I loved to dance.*

I was the ultimate tiny dancer, and let me tell you, I rocked those toe-heels and shuffle-steps. If Instagram had been a thing in 1993, then my class's recital performance of "Put on A Happy Face" would have gone crazy viral. At birthdays and Christmas parties, I forced my family members to sit and watch my one-woman show, while I danced and sang "God Bless America" at the top of my lungs. I could not get enough.

Still, nobody had bothered to tell me that my feet weren't made to dance. Nobody told me dancing wasn't something I should be able to do. Nobody remembered to let me know that I wasn't supposed to be good enough.

Yes, I noticed that my feet didn't always seem to cooperate like the other students' feet did. And I noticed that some of the dance moves took me longer to learn. But it wasn't until I was roughly seven years old that a teacher made the fatal choice that changed everything. Her words shifted my view of myself as a dancer...but also my view of myself as a person.

There was one specific dance move that I just could not get my feet to physically understand. This move was called the Shirley Temple, named after the cute, curly-haired childhood sweetheart from the 1930s. It was a combination of toes and heels, and it required more thought than any other tap move. Even when I stared at my teacher's feet, even though I understood in my mind exactly what I needed to do, I couldn't get my feet to follow along.

It's important to be able to do a move by yourself, and my teacher knew this. She lined us up in one straight line, facing the mirror. Quietly but firmly, she stood in front of each of us, one by one, and she instructed us to show her the move. Everyone seemed to get it. Everyone nailed the toes and the heels. Everyone made it look so effortless. And then it was my turn.

"Okay, Kate! Go ahead!"

You guys, I tried. I told my right toe to move, but my left heel made a sound. I told my weight to shift to the left foot, but nothing happened.

I heard my teacher's voice barking commands to me.

"No, do it again."

"*No,* do it *again.*"

"Kate, no. Try harder. Do it again."

Then I watched her face change from smiling to frustration, then to defeat, and finally to disappointment.

As she walked across the room to change the music, I heard her mutter, *"Dang. Some kids just aren't good enough for this class."*

And there it was.

She was the teacher whom I looked up to. She was the adult teaching me the skill that brought me the most joy. She was the woman I wanted to be like. She was my very own superhero. And she had said I wasn't good enough for this class.

And honestly, though she didn't say this, her words translated to say I just wasn't good enough at anything. And I believed her.

Why wouldn't I? I had believed every other word she said, and I didn't question those words, either.

I know now, a solid twenty-four years later, that *I was enough just by showing up.*

I was in a class to *learn* how to dance.

I was expected to make mistakes.

I was not supposed to be perfect right away.

It was entirely normal that I would struggle a bit and then succeed.

I was already enough, just by showing up.

But that's how it works, isn't it? One person makes just one comment, just that one time, and it sticks. It becomes our truth. It becomes our recording.

Think about it with me.

Someone told Lauren that she looked fat when she wore her favorite dress.

Ruthie's sister heard her belting out Taylor Swift in her car, so she said Ruthie should never sing out loud. Ever. Again.

The guy Sammie has been dating pointed out her "love handles." A stranger laughed pointed and out loud while Monica and Ross rocked out "the routine" in the middle of Dick Clark's New Year's Rockin' Eve. (*Friends?* Anyone?)

The sad truth is this: we believe them every time. We listen to their words, and we choose our actions accordingly.

Lauren stopped wearing her favorite dress.

Ruthie doesn't ever sing in front of anyone. Ever.

Sammie is very self-conscious of her body around her boyfriend—or around anyone, for that matter.

We truly believe we are too fat or too thin.

We feel like we are not good enough, not pretty enough, not smart enough.

When we look in the mirror, we see our love handles, stretchmarks, bird legs and scars.

Our skin is either too black or too white.

Our dreams are too big.

So, what do we do? What is the cure for the syndrome of being *Too Much?*

The world will tell you that this is the cure:

Stay small and quiet.

Don't makes waves.

Hold your breath and hope that nobody actually notices that you feel utterly alone.

May I be honest with you? Just writing those words made my soul really sad.

Because it isn't your fault.

It wasn't your fault
But *it is your problem.*

It's not your fault that someone said you sound like a drowning frog when you sing. But it becomes your problem if you believe the lie, and if you stop singing along to Celine Dion's "All Coming Back to Me Now."

It's not your fault that your mom told you to watch what you eat, because the beaus won't come a'callin' for muffin tops. But it becomes your problem if you believe the lie, and if you starve yourself on protein bars and salad with no dressing. It becomes your problem if you believe the lie and never see the true beauty you are.

It's not your fault Pam made you feel "less than" by telling you to go back where you came from, since you are originally from Argentina. But it becomes your problem if try to hide your heritage from someone else's closed mind. My sweet friend, be proud of who you are, where you've been, and where you're from.

It was not my fault that someone said I wasn't good enough for my tap dance class. But it became my problem when I listened to them, when I decided to put my tap shoes away for many years.

I promise you, my friend: everything is about to change. As soon as you listen more carefully to that unbelievably loud recording, you will find it's not nearly as convincing as you always believed.

It's time to tune into the messages worth hearing.

It's time to take your life back.

Remix

What is the biggest lie you've believed?

How has it affected your actions?

Have you ever given up on something that you later regretted?

What was it?

If you could go back and change your choice, would you?

CHAPTER 3

THE RECORDING: "I DON'T BELONG HERE"

I wish that I could be like the cool kids.
'Cause all the cool kids, they seem to fit in.

~ "cool kids" by Echosmith

~ ~ ~

"Warmup time. Let's go, everybody!"

Those were some of the first words that I heard my new tap teacher say, as she clapped her hands to get our attention.

Now, I must tell you, I was no longer seven years old. In fact, I took a long hiatus from tap dancing classes after my nightmare in the dance studio at age seven. I gave it one more try when I was in high school, but as you might imagine, my tap technique was not quite up to snuff. So, as a senior in high school, I was in a class with all 8th graders.

So much fun, right? Not even close.

These girls couldn't even legally drive, but they could flap-ball-change and pullback circles around me. It was not a great experience for my pride, but it was good practice for my tap technique.

I was twenty years old when I met Mrs. Valarie Lippolt Mack, a goddess of a tap teacher. She was basically the

Beyoncé of the tap dance world. She's might be small in stature, but she could command a room with just one word. Everyone listened in awe. We couldn't help ourselves.

Mrs. Mack taught tap dancing at my college, and I decided to take her class—even though I had that pesky recording playing on a loop in my mind, and I was sure I was a terrible tap dancer. Despite my insecurity, I still loved the art of tap, and hey, it was just a college class. If I bombed, I could just chalk it up to needing an extra performing arts credit. Problem solved.

On the first day of class, I stood front and center. (Apparently, I didn't learn anything from my mistake as a bright and shiny seven-year-old.) All I knew was, I am short. Five feet and one inch, to be exact. If I got stuck behind the 5'9" Amazon-women, I wouldn't be able to see anything. So, there I was, front and center.

That recording in my head was so loud. *What are you doing here? Don't you remember?? You don't belong here! You can't tap dance! You're just not good enough for this. Why are you putting yourself through this again?*

Too late. I was here. I was sure other people could hear the things I was telling myself, so I smiled and laughed to try to drown out the doubts. I was ready to try this shuffle-hop-step thing, and ready to fail.

"Okay, let's try some pullbacks!" Ms. Mack called out. (Actually, we called her Smack. When you say "Ms. Mack" seven times fast, it turns into Smack. So that's what we called her.)

Now, for those of you who aren't fluent in tap dance lingo, let me tell you: *pullbacks are no joke.* You basically hoist yourself into the air, slap both of your toes backwards to make a sound, and stay suspended in the air before landing on your toes. No easy feat, my friend.

I realized very quickly that I was not capable of this voodoo-magic tap move, and I deeply and desperately wanted to avoid another dance studio nightmare.

Slowly, like Homer Simpson moving into the bushes, I made my way to the back of class. This was not normal, and Smack knew it. She walked to the back of the class, and she said, "Kate... what are you doing?"

I'd been caught. I'd been found out.

"Smack, you see, those are very hard... and my defying gravity skills haven't manifested yet."

"Let me see," she said.

So, I tried. And I failed.

I failed hard.

I wanted to say, "Seeeeee? I told you so." But I choked back my comment, and I just kind of shrugged.

"Oh, easy!! Bend your knees!!"

What?

"Try it again, and bend your knees!!"

Okay, Smack, you're clearly blind, but I'll try, just for you.

33

So, I tried.

You guys, it worked.

Then I did it again. And it worked, *again*!

And do you know what else? Each time that it worked, that recording in my head got a little bit softer. All I needed was to make one small change, and suddenly I could achieve something that I had convinced myself I couldn't do.

Crazy how that works.

Another day, Smack instructed us to do some other insane voodoo magic, and I heard her call out these terrifying words: "Okay, now faster."

Once again, I began my slow crawl to the back of the studio, because I knew faster wasn't happening. If she let me dance slowly, then I could fake it decently well. But fast? No ma'am. Not today, Satan.

Once again, Smack called my bluff. In front of the entire class she said, "Kate, what are you doing?"

"Smack, I can't do that."

I was sure I couldn't do it, and the recording in my head had returned to full volume.

Smack said, "Everyone, listen up. Stop tapping."

They stopped. Their feet were still. The room was silent.

Here it comes, I thought. *I may as well take my shoes off right now and save her the energy of saying I am not good enough for this class. This all feels so familiar. Oh wait, that's right. It's familiar because I've been here before.*

"How do you tap faster?" Smack softly asked the class.

My classmates answered her with typical—and totally correct—answers. "You tap smaller. You bend your knees. You don't be a dummy."

"Yes," she said, "but more importantly, *you tap faster.* You just do it. You stop making excuses for why you can't, and start accepting why you can."

She turned her attention to me in the way that only Smack can, with her professional eyes and her dreamer spirit.

Her voice was so kind. She said gently, "Come on, Kate. You can tap faster, so stop telling yourself you can't."

And so, you guys, I tapped faster. I completed the moves she had asked us to complete, and I did them at the warp speed she expected. I kept up.

And for the first time since I was seven years old, that recording diminished to a faint whisper.

Oh, sure, it would rear its ugly head from time to time, especially when it came to tap dancing. But I started listening to a new recording. Now, I had the voice of Smack in my mind, gently reminding me, "You tap faster. You stop making excuses for why you can't, and you start accepting why you can."

Have you had the chance to "tap faster," but you told yourself you couldn't?

Now listen, friend. "Tapping faster" is a metaphor I am giving you for doing anything hard. And believe me, I know "tapping faster" is not always that easy. I get it. But I also know this: it's a start. As avid negative recording subscribers, we need a place to begin. We have to start to change frequency of the jam we are listening to in our heads.

Remember, you don't have to eat the whole elephant at once. You can't. Trust me, I've tried to do it all at once: work out, eat well, learn Spanish, write a book, date, clean my car, and keep my cat alive. If you try to "tap faster" in every area all at once, you won't tap at all. You will trip over your feet, fall on your face, and then you'll have to go to the dentist because your front tooth is busted. Nobody has time for that.

Start with one thing. Not ten – not even two – areas of your life. Just one.

You can work out three times a week. You can get your homework done on time. You can say no to that toxic friend who constantly gets you in trouble. When you look in the mirror, you can compliment your body at least once per day.

Make one small change. For example, stop eating doughnuts and substitute a banana instead. (This was a tough one for me to write. I am a sucker for a good Krispy Kreme doughnut)

Remember: it's not your fault that someone gave you those recordings, but it is your problem.

The change must start with you, and it must start now.

You can tap faster.

It starts with you.

Remix

In what area of your life do you wish
that you could "tap faster"?

Does the thought of "tapping
faster" scare you? If so, why?

Is there a teacher or a role model
who has spoken truth to you?

What did they do or say to impact
your journey so far?

CHAPTER 4

THE RECORDING: "I AM TOO MUCH"

Yeah, I got boy problems,
That's the human in me.
Bling Bling
Then I solve 'em,
That's the goddess in me.

~ Lizzo

~ ~ ~

"Girl, calm down."

If I had a nickel for every time someone had told me those words, I would have a ski lodge in Tahoe, a beach house in Maui, a Golden Doodle puppy named Ralphie, and I would own the Detroit Tigers Baseball team.

I have a lot of energy.

It might be less noticeable, except that I also have a "Here-Is-Every-Emotion-I've-Ever-Felt-EVER" resting face.

I am not skilled at hiding my excitement or joy, and that usually translates into a very excited giggle, lots of clapping, and excessive loud noises.

I have always been one to get excited about small things. This probably stems from playing alone so much when I was a kid. If I didn't get excited about the small things in life, then I would never have had anything to be excited about. My life was small, and my joy was big. I still find so much happiness in the little things: click ink pens, wood-burning fireplaces, an acoustic version of a good song, wildflowers, kettle corn, Edison light bulbs, and anything that smells like vanilla, lavender, pine, or fall.

I recently visited South Tahoe, California, and I discovered these massive pinecones outside of my ski lodge. They were as big as my face. Seriously. If I held the pinecone up in front of my head, you would not have been able to see my face. You probably then would have asked why I was holding a pinecone in front of my face, and my answer would have been, "Because! *This pinecone is as big as my face!*" (You get the gist. These were crazy big pinecones.)

You guys, I was a giddy schoolgirl. I may or may not have smuggled a few of them home in my suitcase. They may or may not be sitting on my coffee table as a centerpiece. I can neither confirm nor deny.

It's the little things in life that make me crazy happy.

But this kind of excitement brings judgement from other people. I cannot tell you how many times I have gotten very excited about a pinecone or a puppy or a taco, and suddenly someone next to me will make an offhanded comment along the lines of, "Whoa... chill out there, Ace. It's just a taco."

First of all, a taco is *never* just a taco.

But secondly, a lifetime of these comments starts to accumulate. Each one is like a tiny paper cut. When you get enough paper cuts, over and over and over, you might find that you're bleeding, and you don't know why.

One of the happiest days of my life was my very first show choir competition during my sophomore year of high school. (Yes, I was in a competitive show choir in high school. Yes, I was that nerd. No, I am not sorry.)

That cold January Saturday in 2004 still reigns as the happiest I have ever been. After a lot of years of feeling like I was alone in the world, I was suddenly surrounded by people who were just like me! They were energetic, nerdy, music lovers. They sang out loud and in full voice in front of people. They danced in the hallways and on the sidewalks, to music or silence. These were my people. I had found my tribe.

I don't think I ever stopped moving that day! The energy in my body was electrifying. I wanted to meet as many people as I possibly could, and I wanted to soak it all in. I wanted to remember every detail of this day in history: The Day When I Finally Felt Like I Belonged.

On that day, I also discovered this hard truth: when we find the special something that sets our hearts on fire, we are suddenly and simultaneously set up for ridicule.

My choir mates were annoyed. They told me to "chill out" or "calm down." I had become "too much to handle." I was ridiculed mercilessly by the people who were supposed to be my teammates.

I felt ashamed of my energy and guilty about my excitement. I had gotten out of my box, and I had stretched my joy bigger than my space. Perhaps I should have known better.

I was too much. I was too loud. If I wanted these paper-cuts to stop happening and hurting, then I needed to slow down, settle down, calm down. It was my only hope for fitting in.

So, I learned to get smaller. I learned to swallow my words, turn down the volume, and tune down the joy.

If I stayed quiet and small, then people wouldn't have to tell me to chill out or calm down. If I wanted to be a functioning member of society, if I wanted to be like everyone else, if I held any hope of acceptance, then I needed to stay still and stay quiet.

The worst part is that these paper cuts came from my family, friends, and coworkers—people who claimed to support who I was.

I got a papercut from Mallory when she pointed and laughed as I tried out a new dance move.

I got a papercut from Diana when she said I couldn't sit with them because I was way too loud.

I got a papercut from Jessica when she called me names because I embarrassed her by singing out loud in school.

I got a papercut when Justin asked, "How do you tell someone who is afraid of being too much, that she is being too much?"

> I was too much.
> I was too loud.
> I was an embarrassment.

> (Just typing those statements flares up the papercuts on my heart.)

I was a happy girl. I found joy in so many small things. And until recently, I believed I was wrong for that.

I thought the rules went like this: *Don't tell anyone when you are excited. Don't speak out if you are joyful. Nobody else finds undeniably immense joy in the smell of fresh cut grass, or a super soft fleece blanket, or a seashell on the beach. Stay low. Stay small. That's the only way to survive.*

Keeping yourself small is a full time job. Ya'll... I was tired.

I was tired of being controlled by other people's opinions of me.

I was tired of stifling my joy and energy, due to the off chance that my happiness would make someone uncomfortable.

I was tired of pretending that I wasn't blessed with the gift of finding joy in the smallest things, like lightbulbs, a terrible 80's song, inspirational tank tops, and Chipotle burrito bowls.

I was tired of pretending that my gift was a curse.

After I had my heart broken by someone who flat out said I was too much, I began to see that, if I wanted to survive with my heart intact,I needed to start living unapologetically.

I can't control if people leave my life. I can't go into someone's head, flip this switch, push that button and pull this lever, and suddenly make them like and accept me. I can't control others, nor do I want to. I don't want that kind of responsibility. I only want to take responsibility for me and my choices.

Now, don't get me wrong. I know that there is a time and a place for everything. Even now, as I sit in one of my favorite coffee shops, I am resisting the urge to use my click pen as a microphone to sing along to "I Will Survive." To everyone else, it's background music. But it calls to me, and yet I must resist. This is partly because I know I have to get this chapter done, and can't keep getting distracted by music or cute small children, or the one-woman show

I could be performing right now for this caffeinated and captive audience. But here's the difference: I am resisting the urge because I have stuff I need to do. I am not resisting because I am ashamed of who I am. I am not stopping myself because I am afraid to embarrass those who know me, or because my joy isn't valid. I am choosing to be quiet and focused, and this decision is on MY terms. I am doing it for me, not for anyone else.

What brings you the greatest joy? What makes you want to tap dance on the ceiling and sing from the rooftops? Whatever it is, whatever is resonating in your heart right now, my sweet friend, is a part of *you*. It's a part of your personality, part of your creative makeup that makes you who you are. So, lean into that.

You are not too much—or too little

You are not too loud—or too quiet

You are worthy of love.

You are worthy of real friendships.

You have a unique place that is only yours on this earth, and the world would be so much less beautiful without you.

Press into that voice.

Press into that vision.

You are exactly who you were meant to be.

Stand tall, my friend.

Don't blend in, when you were born to stand out.

Remix

Have you ever felt like the person you are is
just too much—or maybe, not enough?

Who or what made you feel this way?

Have you have been holding back
from trying something new?

Have you kept yourself from
being your greatest self,
all for fear that people would think you were being
too loud or too much—or too *fill-in-the-blank?*

Take a moment to list five things that
people have ridiculed about you.

Now consider how each of those attrib-
utes is actually a really amazing thing about
you. Write those *truths* down, too.

CHAPTER 5

THE RECORDING: "I NEED YOU TO LIKE ME"

I want you to want me.
I need you to need me.
I'd love you to love me.
I'm beggin' you to beg me.

~ Letters to Cleo

~ ~ ~

If there were a club for People Pleasers, I would be the president. We would have t-shirts, buttons, pop-sockets for our phones, and a Facebook group with over two million members. There would be meetups at local coffee shops and restaurants, though it could take a while to pick where to meet, since we would all want to make sure everyone else was happy with the choice. People Pleasers have a hard time making decisions.

One of the worst questions you can ask a People Pleaser is, "What would you like for dinner?" For people like us, that is the question that nightmares are made of.

I know this well. This was my reality.

I am a recovering People Pleaser. I use the word *recovering* because it took me a long time to realize the truth: I can't please everyone.

Nobody can.

Growing up with divorced parents, I wanted to make sure they both were happy with me. I really dislike letting people down, and I hate upsetting anyone, so I would bend over backwards to make sure they were satisfied and pleased. I would go take pictures with my dad, even though I didn't want to. I would try to put on a brave face for my mom when dad would pick me up, even though I just wanted to cry. I thought if I could just keep everyone happy, if I could keep from hurting anyone's feelings, I wouldn't get into trouble. My life was a delicate balancing act. If I could keep all of the plates spinning, if I could keep my balance and not take a single wrong breath, then everyone in my life would be happy.

I remember wanting so badly to belong to the popular crowd. I wanted to go to the movies every Friday night, to wear clothes from the designer stores (not the hand-me-downs from my cousins), and to get invited to their birthday parties and sleepovers. I didn't talk about my love of mystery novels, and I didn't reveal that I sometimes liked to play in my treehouse and pretend I was on a pirate ship. I didn't dare tell anyone that I had actually, truly enjoyed Barney the Dinosaur when I was growing up (because they sang and danced), or that I knew all of the words to the Veggie Tales' song "Cheeseburger" (I still do).

I tried so hard to fit myself into the mould that these other girls had created. I chased down their definition of cool, and I changed myself to match their descriptions.

As I got into high school, I tried to be subtle. If I heard that people were hanging out, I'd casually mention I'd love to be invited. Other friends from elementary had made this transition into the cool club, and they made it look so easy; girls like Anna Rhee and Maria seemed to fit into the popular crowd so effortlessly. But for some reason, I could never get an invite. No matter how hard I tried to fit in, no matter how deeply I longed to be invited, the phone never rang.

Now don't get me wrong, I had some wonderful friends in high school. We weren't getting into trouble or doing anything illegal—which honestly, I see as a blessing now. Had I been accepted into the elite club of the popular girls, I would have been pressured to do things I was not okay with doing, and I am glad I didn't have to make that decision. But my circle of friends? We were not even close to popular. We played chess, baked cookies, and watched Star Wars on Saturday nights. We weren't cool, but we had a lot of fun.

Still, I had this ache in my heart to fit in. I wanted to be popular. I wanted everyone to like me.

This wasn't just a high school hope. When I got to college, I was in a show choir that performed all over the

Midwest. I thought this could be my big break into the popular crowd.

I wanted so badly to fit in. I wanted the other girls to like me. I didn't want to be too much to handle. I didn't want to mess up. So, I held my breath, I tried, and I failed to fit in. I couldn't stifle my love of music and performing just because I didn't want to be ridiculed like I was in high school.

Most of these girls weren't even nice. I watched them tear down others and talk behind people's backs. I didn't want to be like them, but I was so tired of always being on the outside. I just wanted to be liked. I wanted to be accepted.

So, I tried a new approach.

I went to the parties. I had the drinks, even though I was terrified of alcohol. My only experience with any kind of booze was my drunken father, and that was no happy time, I assure you. I wore the skirts that were shorter than I was comfortable with. I said the curse words that I had never used. I put myself into situations that weren't good or healthy, all in the name of fitting in and being accepted. I suppressed who I was to make sure I was invited to another party, accepted in the crowd who watched the Tony Awards.

I wasn't fulfilled. I wasn't gratified.

I was empty. But I was *in*.

One particular "mean girl" was the leader of the pack, and we will call her Jonnie. She was loud and flamboyant, and she was so popular. She would tear someone down at a soulful level, and then hug them and tell them she loved them. When I look back now, I can see how deeply she hurt people with this abusive pattern, and yet we all craved those words from her. Everyone wanted her love and approval, even though she was mean and degrading.

The People Pleaser in me wanted nothing more than to be her best friend.

I achieved that status for a short amount of time. She confided some very personal information to me, and that was the moment: I knew I had made it. Jonnie and I went on McDonald's runs, and we drove to Wichita at 3am for a Krispy Kreme fix. We watched musicals together, and we laughed at people who weren't as talented as she was.

I had made it. I was at the top of the pyramid. My name was at the top of the most popular girl's list.

I found joy in it... briefly. I had no idea how fleeting it could be.

Her birthday party landed on the same night as a formal dance, and I made a fatal choice when I missed her party. That decision knocked me right off the top of the pyramid, and she made sure I crashed hard. Not only did she end our friendship, but she spent the entire evening slandering my name, telling everyone that I was a terrible person. She blacklisted me in our circle of friends, and I wasn't even allowed inside the football stadium anymore if her friends were also there.

Everything I had worked for, all those nights of trying to fit the mold she required: wasted.

Once again, I didn't belong anymore. I was crushed.

All I craved was approval. Yes, I wanted Jonnie's approval, but I wanted the other girls to like me, too. But when Jonnie made up her mind, nobody dared say anything different. I was back to square one, and it hurt. I was lonely and devastated. But I couldn't force anyone to like me. I couldn't change them.

I could only change me... and the way I thought about myself.

Luckily, all of this happened as I was transferring to a new university. I met new friends—real friends—and I left behind the dust of Jonnie and the other mean girls. Now I can see how toxic she was, but realities like this are so hard to see in the moment. I was so focused on needing people to like me, on needing to fit in, that I subjected myself to terrible treatment by people who didn't deserve my attention.

It is so easy, especially us People Pleasers, to bend and twist and mold ourselves to fit in where we never belonged in the first place.

I have invested years in surrounding myself with truly good people who have built me up instead of tearing me down, and now I realize an important key truth: I didn't need to please anyone. If I was pleased with myself, I exuded an inner peace that good people find attractive. These are the people who deserve a voice in my life.

The only person I can change is myself. And at the end of the day, the only person I must answer to is me. (Well, and probably my mother, but that's a whole other cup of tea).

I needed to get right with myself so I could truly find the value and joy in who I am. This journey took years of trial and error, but I finally began to learn this truth: I am most content and attractive to others when I am at peace with myself.

Everyone has an invite to join me in my journey through this life, but not everyone accepts that invitation. And you know what? That is totally okay. I have learned that I can't always get everyone to like me, but I can always be kind. I may not be everyone's cup of tea, but I can always show love.

And if someone is a jerk, it was one-hundred-percent okay for me to walk away from them. (Jesus said to turn the other cheek, but he didn't say to stand there and let them beat the crap out of you.)

I get to make my choices, and I choose to be kind to myself and to others.

And that?

Well, that makes me somebody worth inviting to the Tony Awards.

Remix

Was there ever a time that you
felt you didn't belong?

Do you have a *Jonnie* in your life?

How did you change yourself to earn
their approval? Was it worth it?

What are some ways that you can start to separate
yourself from the negative voices in your life?

What kind of people do you want
to walk through life with you?

What can you change in yourself to
make you a friend worth choosing?

CHAPTER 6

THE RECORDING: "I HAVE TO FIT IN"

Don't laugh at me, don't call me names.
Don't get your pleasure from my pain.

~ "Don't Laugh at Me" by Mark Wills

~ ~ ~

I am not trying to brag, but I can fit inside of a tuba band locker.

Yes, you read that correctly.

I, Kate Ellen Garnes, have scrunched my body to fit inside of a high school band locker designed to hold a tuba.

I can also fit inside of most regulation-sized trash cans. I did not find this out just for the heck of it, like the time when I folded myself into a clothes dryer just to prove I could. The band locker was different.

I was stuffed in there by the high school senior boys. They did it because it was funny.

They thought it was funny to pick me up—the girl who was smaller than their other classmates—and put me somewhere I couldn't get out of on her own. The boys thought it was even more hilarious to watch me try to fight back to defend myself, all to no avail. Their laughter didn't stop when I gave up fighting back and just let it happen. They thought it was funny.

So, I laughed.

I laughed hard.

I was still laughing when I was late for choir because I couldn't get out of the tuba locker. In fact, I was only released from my instrumental prison cell because I laughed loud enough for someone to hear me.

I belly-laughed louder than the recording blaring in my head, the message telling me that I wasn't worth rescuing, that I was less valuable than a tuba.

Of course, I laughed. Remember? That is what I had trained my body to do.

I had trained my emotions to laugh when I was feeling anything less than joy. It was much easier to giggle at the boys who closed the locker, than to tell them that I didn't find it funny at all. When I told them to stop and put me down, it was easier to just laugh it off than to feel the hurt when they ignored me. I finally surrendered all together. My opinion didn't matter. My feelings were not important. There was nothing I could do.

So, I laughed.

You guys, it sucks to get picked on, even if it's "in good fun."

Actually, let's get one thing clear: it's not "fun" to become the butt of a joke.

Most people do not enjoy having their flaws spotlighted and laughed about. Nobody enjoys that. There's actually a name for this kind of incessant teasing. It's called *Bullying*.

Listen, can I be really honest right now? I hate that word. There is such a fabricated stigma behind it.

Let's think about this. When you think of a bully, you probably picture a big kid with a face like Sid from the Toy Story movies. You probably picture someone who steals someone's lunch money or pushes kids off the swings. Maybe you picture the super-popular girl who wears pink and writes awful things about people in a "burn book." Maybe you envision Ms. Trunchbolt, the teacher from Matilda, when she throws kids across the room by their pigtails. Maybe you picture your boss, the superior for whom your work never seems to be good enough. They accuse you of being lazy, dumb, or ignorant if you miss a memo or a deadline.

You get the picture. We all have an example in our head of what a bully looks like.

But here's the deal, and here's the reason why I hate that word: we don't recognize the true bullies.

You probably don't think a close friend is "bullying" when she says you're stupid because you didn't pass a test. You probably don't think the guy at the gym is "bullying" when he laughs when because you can't bench press your bodyweight. You probably don't think your mom is "bully-ing" when she takes you to Weight Watchers because she fears you will never land a guy if you don't lose those few extra pounds.

When the bully is someone close to you, when the bully is someone who is supposed to love you unconditionally, then we call it "tough love." That's all.

It couldn't be bullying, right? Never. That hurts too much.

You know what else we don't recognize as "bullying?" Society Let's consider the messages society sends to us every single day. If you aren't in the popular circle, there must be something wrong with you.

If you don't get more than fifty likes on a post, there must be something wrong with you.

If you don't dress like everyone else, there must be something wrong with you.

If you are single, there must be something wrong with you.

If you're not married before you turn thirty, there must be something wrong with you.

Society is the biggest bully of all.

Society feeds us lies every single day. Lies like these:

Men can't cry or show emotion.

Women were made to be in the kitchen and raise the kids, not to create companies or change the world.

College is the only way to be successful, and if we don't go, we will be just like our dead-beat ancestors.

Salad, rice cakes, and six-minute-mile runs are the only ways to truly love the body you see in the mirror.

Mental illness is weakness. And if you go to a therapist, you're crazy.

Keep your head down and work hard. Don't make waves. If you follow all the rules, then maybe in fifty years, you will find the success you seek.

The saddest part about these lies? They feel so true. Society is very good at hitting us exactly where it hurts, but it delivers these lies with a wink and a smile. And we believe every word.

Society is the biggest bully of all. Society sends mixed messages that are hard to understand. Be different, but be sure to fit in.

Be tough, but stay humble.

Be seen, but don't stand out.

Be unique, but don't be an outcast.

Fight back, but make peace.

Stay thin, but be healthy.

Oh, and don't worry, if you ever feel like you're not quite up to snuff in any one of those categories, society will give you a filter, a diet, an app, a program, or a pill. Society will tell you what to do, and then society will give you a remedy to fix all of your "problems."

Society is the biggest bully of all.

Consider this.

If we replaced the word "society" with the name of a person, maybe "Brenda" or "Austin," then you and I would agree that Brenda and Austin are pretty huge bullies. They are mean. Their words hit where it hurts. They pinpoint our weaknesses with cruel specificity.

But this bully's name is not "Brenda" or "Austin."

It's society.

Society is the biggest bully of all.

I don't know about you, but the thought of trying to stand up against society or the social norms? Well, that seems harder than winning the hardest level of Rainbow Road in Mario Kart 64! It seems harder than trying to lick my own elbow.

Listen, I get it. It's not easy—not even a little bit. Just typing the society's lies makes me feel exhausted in my heart, soul, and spirit.

So, what if—and just go with me on this—what if we stopping giving everyone and everything else the power? What if you and I choose to become truly okay with being in our own skin? Society isn't going to stop screaming at us, but we don't have to listen. What if you and I can turn all of those lies turn into white noise?

Why are we trying so hard to fit in, when we were born to stand out?

Why are we stuffing ourselves into boxes, stereotypes, labels, trashcans—and band lockers— where we were never meant to be in the first place?

Instead, we can give our focus and our energy to the people who build us up. We can give our attention to the dreams we can achieve. If we can't silence the "bully," at least we can turn it into white noise.

It won't be easy. But it could change everything.

(Also: Ten points to those of you who tried to lick your elbow a few paragraphs ago. Well done, my friends.)

Remix

What lies you have you heard from a "bully" in your life? or by society?

If you could make any of those lies into "white noise," what lies would you silence?

CHAPTER 7

THE RECORDING: "STAY IN YOUR LANE"

"Please stand clear of the doors.
Por favor mantenga alejado de las puertas."

- The Walt Disney World Monorail

~ ~ ~

Way back in middle school, when it was time to choose a language to study, everybody I knew chose to study Spanish. So, naturally, I chose to study French.

With the wisdom of a couple of decades, I wish now that I could have a very serious conversation with Ninth Grade Kate, and I would tell her not to worry so much about being a non-conformist. Just take the dang Spanish class. But Ninth Grade Kate didn't know I would be moving to Florida in just a few years, and she didn't know that speaking Spanish would become a useful skill.

Growing up in Missouri, I didn't know many native Spanish speakers. Actually, I didn't know anyone for whom English was even their second language. I wasn't intentionally sheltered, but there just wasn't a sizable Hispanic population in central Missouri. So perhaps you can imagine my confusion when I moved to Florida and encountered a billboard that was written completely in Spanish.

I had never come across a road sign that I couldn't read. I felt ignorant and confused. I felt inexperienced and uneducated. And I hated it.

I decided to get to the roots of the culture here in Orlando. I wanted to learn more about my Spanish-speaking friends in this new city. So, I did what I do: I asked questions. I read books. I watched videos. I chose different music choices. I went salsa dancing.

And I fell in love.

What a vivacious culture! I was blown away by the music, the food, the passion, the family traditions—all of it. Everything felt so different from the culture I had grown up in, and I had a brand-new appreciation for the differences in other people's upbringings, beliefs, and customs.

Learning about the Spanish-speaking culture was suddenly not enough. I wanted to speak the language. I wanted to show my friends that their heritage mattered, their language mattered—they mattered.

My next step: I got Rosetta Stone, a software package for learning a new language.

Now if you've never used something like Rosetta Stone, let me give you a quick heads up: you will feel ridiculous. The technology requires you to speak into a computer, and then a buzzer sounds when you say something incorrectly. If you're anything like me, that buzzer went off basically

THE RECORDING: "STAY IN YOUR LANE"

every time I opened my mouth! The whole process will humble you to your core, but if you stick with it, you can find some incredible results. But don't say I didn't warn you.

The most ideal place for me to practice Spanish was in my bedroom, alone where nobody could hear me, but I couldn't stay home all the time to learn my new language. The whole game changed when I would attempt to practice in a room full of people. I wish I could say that I am the type of person who doesn't care what people think about my newfound hobby and the learning curve, but I am not that person.

See, I really dislike making people uncomfortable by intruding into their space. If listening to music will interrupt someone else's silence, then I won't turn it on because I don't want to bother them. If I am in a really quiet room, I won't bust open a bag of potato chips and start crunching and munching, because I know just how annoying it can be to hear someone chew their food. When someone is speaking to me, I try not to look at my phone, yawn, or zone out for even a second, because I don't want them to think I don't care. I really dislike making people upset or uncomfortable.

So, it was an inch or two outside my comfort zone when I decided to take my laptop into work so I could practice Spanish on my off time. I determined to be as quiet as possible, and that's partly why I kept hearing that buzzer. I

71

was speaking so softly that the computer couldn't tell what I was trying to say.

Some cast members and I were scattered around a small breakroom in between shows, and I had settled myself into a tiny corner of the room to get some Spanish practice in. Unfortunately, I picked the wrong breakroom on the wrong day with the wrong people.

A girl (we will call her Ruthie) noticed me in my quiet corner with my incorrect pronunciations, my buzzing computer, and my embarrassment. In front of God and everyone in the entire breakroom, she loudly proclaimed, "Do you know what is the most annoying thing you can do in a breakroom? Try to learn Spanish."

Ouch.

Oh, man. I had done it. I had made people uncomfortable, and now they were laughing. I should have known better. I slid right into Apology Mode as I shut down my computer. "Oh, I am sorry!! I'll try to be quieter. I have to go do a show anyway."

I left the breakroom with a flicker of hope that this was the last I would hear of the choice I had made. These people were notorious for creating satirical posts and pictures on social media to embarrass the people we worked with, and I had been lucky enough to escape their scrutiny... so far. I would simply have to find a new hiding spot for my secret Spanish lessons.

In the breakroom after the show, just as I was about to get my wallet and grab some lunch, I heard someone say, "Hey Kate, check your Facebook."

Uh-oh.

"I am actually headed to get some lunch. I'll be back," I stammered.

"No, girl... seriously. Check your Facebook."

I felt nauseous. I pulled my phone out of my pocket, and I opened my Facebook.

My profile photo had been photoshopped.

The image of my face now had a goatee, thick eyebrows, and a bandana.

All around my face were the words "buscando trabajo," which means *looking for work.*

They had captioned the photo, "Saw this standing outside of the Home Depot."

Everyone was laughing.

My hands were shaking, and I felt a lump in my throat.

I started to laugh to hide my shame. I laughed all the way down the hallway, just in case anyone followed me to the cafeteria. Once I knew I was alone, I broke. I cried. I couldn't fight the wave of shameful tears that were pouring from my eyes.

Why was I so embarrassed? Because I couldn't turn down the volume of a fresh, new recording that was saying, "Who do you think you are, trying to better yourself? Trying to learn Spanish? Yeah, right. Stay in your lane, Kate. Don't try to rise above your level. Stop trying to be someone you aren't. Nobody wants you to speak to them in Spanish. You are a fraud. You are a hack. Stay in your lane."

The shame recording was so painful that I couldn't bring myself to even open my computer, much less to open Rosetta Stone. The lies sounded like truths. And I believed them.

I quit studying Spanish. And I refused to tell anyone that I had ever even thought about trying to learn Spanish.

A few months later, my dear friend Melanie noticed something was off with me, and she wasn't about to let me off the hook.

"Kate, how's your Spanish going? I haven't seen you with your computer in a while."

I tried to divert the conversation, but she wasn't stupid. She knew me better than that. I wasn't going to get off the hook that easily. (We all need friends who won't let us off the hook.)

"What happened?" she asked.

I hung my head in shame. I didn't want to have to admit the truth, that I had tried to dream bigger than the lane I was given. I didn't want to talk about it. I spoke softer than normal. I refused to make eye contact. I wanted to cry. But I told her, nonetheless.

She was furious. (We all need friends who will get furious when others wrong us.)

"Oh Kate," she said, "I am angry. I am angry that anyone would treat you that way. I am angry that someone would let their own insecurity allow them to be so racist and hateful. But I will tell you right now, you are better than that. In fact, I don't ever want to see you without your computer again. I am going to text you in Spanish, and I expect you to respond to me in Spanish. You will not let one post, not one photo, not one word of one person stop you from reaching hundreds of people."

Mic. Drop.

Melanie was the first person to put an abrupt stop to my recording. Her truth made me feel like I had been hit by a truck, and yet also lifted on a cloud. She was right. I had allowed one person and one post to stop me from bettering myself. Did I actually feel shame for trying to learn how to speak to people who spoke a different language? Yeah, actually, I had. But I would be damned if I let it happen again.

I am eternally grateful for Melanie, for the fact that she loved me enough to help me hear beyond my recording. She helped me see that it was a lie. I had every right to be so proud of myself for trying to help others feel welcome, and I should feel pride in the fact that I was taking steps to reach those I couldn't have reached before. Not only did

I need to break out of my lane, but I needed to take over the *whole dang highway!*

Have you ever done something like this? I mean, we kind of do it all the time, right?

We get so afraid of hurting others, fearful of making people uncomfortable, that we stifle our own growth.

We stay low because other people are too afraid to stand up.

We stay silent because others are too afraid to speak out.

We lower our standards because other people are too scared to raise theirs.

You guys, no longer.

I will not apologize for trying to better myself.

I will not dim my light anymore, because people are too afraid to brighten theirs.

And neither will you.

You are worth far more than the lies you have been told.

You are bigger than the lane you have always known.

You are worth learning Spanish.

You are worth achieving any goal.

Turn on your turn signal, and get ready to take over any lane you would like to drive in.

Buckle up.

We're going on a road trip.

Remix

Have you ever stopped pursuing a dream
because of someone's comment?

Is there something you have delayed in
your life, all for fear of dreaming too big?

Write a book?
Forgive someone who wronged you?
Run a Marathon?
Audition for Big Brother?
Go back to college?

What would it take to claim your
truth and begin again?

What types of things are you posting or following on social media?
Are your posts filled with negativity or sarcasm?
What can you do to fill your social media
channels with kindness and hope?

CHAPTER 8

THE RECORDING: "EVERYONE ELSE HAS IT FIGURED OUT"

I can see a new horizon,
Underneath a blazing sky.
I'll be where the eagle's flying high and higher.

~ "St. Elmo's Fire"

~ ~ ~

At my ten-year high school reunion, I was sad. Like, really sad.

I was surrounded by hundreds of people with whom I had trudged through high school. Together, we battled acne, Bosco cheese sticks, Mrs. Shumate's awful-hard Geometry class, Friday night football games, pep rallies, senior pranks, prom, and graduation. We experienced more than a few heartbreaks together, including the sudden loss of fellow classmates. For a lot of years, they were my people.

Somehow, ten years later, it seemed I was the only one—and I do mean the ONLY one—not married with a couple of kids and a "grownup" job. You see, when you grow up in the Midwest, that is the path that is expected of you. After high school graduation, you're supposed to go to college, get married, have two babies, and become a middle school art teacher. You get the dog, the white picket fence, and the 401K. If you don't have those things, then something must be totally wrong with you.

(Need I remind you: my situation was further complicated by the fact that I was a professional performer at the time, so it appeared that I made my living by playing dress-up.)

I had the high school diploma and the college degree, but I had no husband, no kids, and no fat diamond ring on my finger. After about two hours of small talk—about how cute Addy's baby is, how handsome Holly's husband is, how accomplished the McNut twins are, and how Brian couldn't be here because he's helping poor orphan kids with cancer in Uganda—I was done.

I sat down at a table by myself, I sipped my drink, and I had myself a nice little Pity Party for One. I ripped myself apart, questioning every decision I'd ever made. I mean, even the nerdy kids from high school were married. What the heck did I do wrong?

Lacey Phillips plopped down next to me, and the small talk began again. Lacey was the perfect girl in high school. She had great grades, she was very funny, she was a soloist in the choir, and she was in the popular crowd. Basically, she was everything I wanted to be.

After high school, Lacey had faced her own very hard situations, and her honesty paved the way for a different kind of conversation. I admitted the truth to Lacey. I was bummed out. I felt less than adequate.

Then, Lacey said ten words that would change my life forever. She asked,

"Well, what do you want your life to look like?"

Someone was brave enough to ask me a hard question. Someone was brave enough to interrupt my pity party with an honest question. I said the words out loud and my life hasn't been the same since. You see, words have the power to build and to destroy. Words have the power to lift and to tear down. Throughout my life, words of others have killed my dreams or sparked my joy. They have brought tears of happiness or tears of complete devastation.

When Lacey asked me that question, something inside me flipped. Some may call it the universe, the force, or energy. I call it God. In that moment, God started me on my adventure. She asked a question, and I knew the answer. I had never spoken my dream out loud before, and as soon as I did, something inside me shifted.

"I want to be a motivational speaker."

You know when you get inside your car, and your windows are foggy, so you turn on the de-fog? And everything is foggy, until all of the sudden, your windshield becomes crystal pinpoint clear? That is the best way to describe what happened in my head at that exact moment.

As soon as I said it out loud, something inside me shifted. Those words changed me, and I had never been more convicted of anything in my entire life. That question would change my entire path on this earth.

Fast forward a year and a half. Thousands of dollars in coaching and training. Hundreds of hours preparing my talk. A dozen times that I gave up because I was sure I wasn't good enough. A dozen more times that I felt convicted all over again. I knew what to do with my life, and my moment had come. I was a motivational speaker on the lunch rotation stage at the National Student Council Convention in Minnesota.

I had worked so hard for this moment, and I still wasn't entirely sure why anyone would listen to me. I didn't know why they would want to hear my story, but I told it anyway. I listened to the new recording I had created for myself.

I was a gladiator.

I was made for more.

I had a story to tell, and people needed to hear it.

I had a purpose.

I listened. I believed it.

After my second talk of the day, most of the students had left the auditorium, but one sweet girl and her friend stayed back to speak with me.

As they walked up, I realized immediately that something was different about this girl. She only said, "Thank you. I don't know how you knew, but thank you."

She hugged me, and she cried while I hugged her back. In that moment I knew, this is why I was put on this earth.

My purpose was not to be the laughingstock of the performing arts department.

My purpose was not to be stuffed into lockers.

My purpose was not to get my heart broken into a million pieces by a jerk.

My purpose wasn't the lies I had told myself for years and years, about not being a good enough daughter, dancer, singer, teacher or choreographer.

My purpose became clear.

My purpose is to bring hope to teenagers and adults, to show them the truth: your recordings are not the end of your story. You can choose carefully the words you hear.

I had made it to the other side, and I had stepped into my purpose without shame or fear. I started truly believing the battle cry I had sounded so many years ago. I was no longer defined by the things I hadn't done, or by things I might never do. I was no longer bound by the opinions of others, especially those peasants in the cheap seats.

I had found my purpose. I had found my calling.

And so can you.

Had I listened to the naysayers or the doubters or the "just kidding" friends, I never would have stepped out of my comfort zone and found my true passion. I would have continued to truly believe I was a failure. I would have believed I'd never amount to anything. I would have continued to listen to the negative recordings I had grown to know. I would have continued living a life I wasn't meant to live.

I am meant to live a life of happiness and joy. I am meant to help others on their journey. I am meant for more. And so are you.

You are meant for more. You are meant to live a life of happiness and joy. You are meant to literally change the world. But the change starts with you. It starts with your thoughts. It begins with the ways you speak to yourself. You see, your words to yourself affect how you speak to the world, which in turn affects the world around you. Do you want to live in darkness surrounded by people who tear you down, and lie to you? Then keep doing what you're doing. But if you dream of more, then hang on tight. Your life is about to change in ways you never thought possible.

I'll be honest, it's not easy. In fact, it's really hard to win the battle of your thoughts. But as soon as you do, you'll start to see your life shift in ways. You'll start to believe in beauty and love again. You'll find your purpose.

Remix

What in your life makes you come alive?

Have you ever set a goal for yourself and achieved it?

What did that feel like?

What if you could achieve all your goals
and come out on the other side?

How does that thought make you feel?

CHAPTER 9

THE RECORDING: "I DON'T NEED HELP"

Help me if you can, I am feeling down.
And I do appreciate you being around.
Help me get my feet back on the ground.
Won't you please, please help me?

~ "Help" by The Beatles

~ ~ ~

One of the best videos to grace the internet is a 46-second video of a little girl who can't be more than two years old. This sweet girl is sitting in the backseat of the car, attempting to buckle the car seat all by herself—and to no avail.

Her father is in the front seat, and he has the camera poised and ready, since this is clearly not the first time this situation has presented itself. He keeps asking his sweet daughter, "Would you like some help?"

"No, thank you. I do it myself."

She is very obviously struggling, and any adult can see that she actually cannot do this herself, even if she is trying her hardest.

Through muffled laughter, the dad asks patiently, "What can I do?"

89

The two-year-old replies, without missing a beat, "Worry about yourself. You DRIVE! No, thank you, worry about yourself."

I love it every time.

Any of us who has tried to buckle a tiny human into one of these car seats knows:... this is no easy feat. Even those of us with the most skilled of buckling abilities still have trouble jamming the little metal buckle into the hook just right, without pinching our fingers, or getting stuck like a Chinese finger trap. But she was determined to buckle it herself. She would not ask for help. She would not admit defeat.

I am sad that this is where the video ends. I would have watched for another two minutes to know how this situation played out. Did the dad continue to just let her struggle while she figured it out herself? Did she finally give in and admit she might not be able to handle this one today? The world may never know.

What I do know is this: I resonate with the effort of this two-year-old on a spiritual level.

The world I grew up in wasn't quite as instant as today's world. Today, people don't even have to get out of their cars to do their grocery shopping, and they can have a doctor's appointment online without ever leaving the comfort of the living room couch. Everything is instant. Instant

THE RECORDING: "I DON'T NEED HELP"

coffee. Instant messaging. Instant responses. Instant news. Instant gratification. Don't get me wrong—it's nice most of the time. We can find most of our answers without ever having to actually admit to anyone that we have a question.

But when I grew up, not everything was instant. You had to look words up in a dictionary if you didn't know how to spell it. (Which doesn't make a lot of sense, since you have to know how to spell it to look it up.) If you were driving somewhere unfamiliar, you had to use an atlas with maps that you hoped were up-to-date.

You know what else wasn't instant? Trying to reach the box of cereal that is on the top shelf at the grocery store, when you are only five feet tall.

I have always disliked asking for help. It always felt like I was admitting that I wasn't smart or capable enough to figure something out on my own. The absolute worst situation involved having to ask someone who was taller than me to reach the box of Captain Crunch that was too high for me to get on my own. This was my very last option I would ever choose, and only after I had already tried everything I could do myself—including climbing up the shelves of a dozen other cereals. I did anything I could to avoid asking for any sort of assistance.

I have a firm policy: I can reach it myself. I can figure it out myself. I can handle it myself. I can fight for myself.

I can exhaust myself while doing it all myself. You worry about yourself. I can do it myself.

See, just asking for help has never really been *just asking for help*.

Asking for help meant I was too weak to handle it myself.

Asking for help meant I didn't have all the answers.

Asking for help meant I had to reveal that I didn't know the answer.

Asking for help meant I wasn't smart enough, capable enough, or strong enough to do it on my own.

Asking for help admitted weakness and failure.

Asking for help was unacceptable.

I suspect I am not alone in this, right? When a stranger notices that you're struggling to handle all of your groceries since you didn't grab the cart on the way in and now you keep dropping everything, you probably kindly say, "No, thank you, I am good thanks!"

We become blinded by our refusal to admit that we might not be able to do everything on our own. We are so focused on holding our breath to keep all the plates spinning, keep everyone happy, keep the details moving, that we don't realize we are exhausting ourselves in the name of "I've got this" and "I can handle this" and "I am fine—everything is fine—*I am totally fine.*"

We aren't totally fine. We don't have it all together. We don't have everything figured out. And we can't do it all ourselves.

We try so hard to keep from drowning that we can't see the hand that's been extended to us.

Asking for help also meant that I had to admit a painful truth: I couldn't do everything asked of me. See, I had a bad case of the "of course" syndrome. Have you ever sounded like this?

"Of course I can take you to the airport after only two hours of sleep because of my other job."

"Of course, I can take care of your dog for two weeks while you travel, even though I know absolutely nothing about dogs."

"Of course I can make another two batches of cookies for this bake sale at your school, even though I really hate baking. Oh, yes, of course I refuse to be the only one bringing in store-bought cookies."

"Of course I can help you with this situation, even though I am struggling to breathe myself."

"Of course I won't say no when you ask for help, because I can do this."

"Of course I can handle this, and I can handle that. What's one more hour of work? What's one more appointment? What's one more meeting?"

can handle it. I can cover it. I can bake it. I can create it. I'll sleep next week. I'll eat later. I'll cry when I get a chance to breathe. I just need a little bit more coffee. Of course.

I mean, everybody else can do it, right? We spend our days looking at Rachel's Instagram with her perfect nails, perfect children, perfect husband, perfect dog, and perfectly prepared dinner. We see Julie's Pinterest walls filled with all her DIY creations, from her children's Halloween costumes to her totally organic dog treats. We see Karen's photos of her totally perfect six-pack-abs that she got because she created her own workout using only the things in her kitchen.

I am sure none of *them* asked for help. Look at how *they* have it all together.

There is no fine print on Instagram to say that Rachel has a full team in her house to help keep her family, career, and lifestyle clean and tidy. Nowhere is it posted that Julie spent hours and hours in classes learning how to create different craft projects, so that she wouldn't cry herself to sleep at night anymore feeling like a failure. Karen doesn't post about the personal trainer she hired to help her create this workout in her own home, or that she has gone into crippling debt to keep this image.

We truly believe that none of these women asked for help. Of course they didn't, because in our recording, asking for help is a failure.

When we fail, when all of the plates come crashing down around us, we blame ourselves. We say things like, *I wasn't good enough. I didn't try hard enough. I didn't sacrifice enough. Next time I will just have to try harder. Nobody else is to blame but myself. I need to put my head down, swallow the tears, and work harder. I don't need anyone's help. I can do this myself.*

Asking for help has gathered a terrible reputation. But what if we flipped the script?

Instead of seeing it as a weakness or as a cop out, what if we saw it as a strength? When did it become taboo to want to learn something new?

When you hit rock bottom surrounded by the shards of all of the spinning plates that have since fallen and shattered on the ground, you have nowhere to go but up. But have you ever tried to get out of a hole completely by yourself? You get dirty and bruised and bloody when you're trying to claw, scratch and dig your way out. We ignore the hands offering to help pull us up because of the insistence, "I don't need help," or "I can handle this."

My sweet friend, accepting help is not a weakness.

Asking for help is not a cop out.

Accepting help means you are admitting you have things to learn, and you are humble enough to be the student. When you allow someone to help you, you are loving yourself enough to know your limits. You are loving yourself well enough to stop trying to do what is humanly impossible.

Don't get me wrong—I am still working on this recording. I am just like that little two-year-old in the video. I have a strong pattern of, "I've got this. I can handle this. Sure, I can do anything for you while sacrificing my sanity, happiness, sleep, and solitude." It took me a long time to realize that asking for help was actually a type of self-love I had never known. I didn't have to have it all figured out. It didn't make me any less of a woman, speaker, dancer, friend, or daughter for me to say I didn't have all the answers and to admit that I might need some guidance.

When I started my journey as a professional speaker in 2016, I knew that I had absolutely zero clue what I was doing. I didn't know how to start. And I knew I was way out of my league. So, I humbled myself enough to be honest: if I was going to commit to this, I needed to seek out help. I needed to admit I didn't have all the answers, and I needed someone to guide me. That's when I was led to my speaking coach, Harriet. One of the first things I said to her was, "I have no idea what I am doing. I have no idea if I'll even be good at this. But I know you are the best of the best, and I trust your guidance. So, forgive all of the questions I am going to ask, and the insecurities that are going to come screaming out. If you'll help me, I promise I will be a sponge and soak it all up."

When you ask someone humbly for their wisdom or guidance, they are almost always excited and ready to assist. People like feeling wise. People like feeling impor-tant. Most people are honored that you want their opinion, guidance, or lessons. Some people won't want to help you, and you know what? That's okay. Let those folks go, and let it roll off your back. I can promise you this: theirs isn't the wisdom you wanted in the first place.

We can't do everything ourselves, as much as we would love to. We all dream of being a superhero, saving the world, and being able to do it all ourselves. Even super-heroes have help. They have a side kick, a British butler, or a fellow superhero. They call for back up when needed.

Asking for help when you've hit the end of your rope? That's what I call courage.

Strength, to me, looks like admitting we need assistance.

Vulnerability is asking someone taller to reach the cereal on the top shelves at the grocery store.

I am giving you permission, today, my sweet friend, to call for backup. Send up a smoke signal for reinforcements. Sound the alarm and rally the troops. You don't have to do everything yourself anymore. You can love yourself enough to admit you need some help. That is not a weakness, that is an extreme strength.

Stop trying to keep all the plates spinning. Stop trying to scale the shelves at the supermarket. Stop trying to do it all. You weren't meant to. You were meant to do your best, and your best is absolutely enough. Your best doesn't mean driving yourself into the ground to frost the perfect cupcakes. Your best doesn't mean fainting from exhaustion after you've accepted too many to-do's and assignments. Your best is taking care of yourself and allowing others to help you with the rest.

I wish I could hug that sweet little two-year-old from the video. I would tell her how proud I am of her for being brave enough to try things on her own. I would tell her that she is beautiful, and I would tell her that this achiever spirit will take her really far in life. I would then tell her that sometimes, it's okay to let her daddy help. It's okay to let people help us when something might just be a bit too much, or when we might be in over our heads. She's going to take over the world someday, and I can't wait to see it happen, but she won't do it alone.

And she doesn't have to. Sometimes, she may need to ask for help.

Remix

Think of a time when you needed
help, but you didn't ask for it.

What was the main reason you held back?
How does it feel to you to ask for help?

Is it scary? Is it empowering? Does
it feel like a weakness?

How can you shift your perspective to a
position of strength and courage?

Challenge for you: Ask for help with something once a day for a month. Don't back down
or quit on yourself. Seek out guidance on one
thing every day. Notice how your life shifts.
Notice how your relationships have grown.

At the end of the month, ask yourself, what
was the biggest shift you felt when you
started actively seeking guidance or help?

CHAPTER 10

THE RECORDING: "I HAVE NOTHING LEFT TO GIVE"

"We are out gunned, out manned,
outnumbered, out planned."

- Hamilton

~ ~ ~

I. Hate. This.

During my senior year of college, I said those words every single day. I was a music education major with no desire to become a music teacher. The trajectory was not good.

Now, don't get me wrong. I loved music. I loved teenagers. I loved to motivate. The art of teaching was a skill I dreamed of having. I tried to love it. I really tried.

But, by golly, I *hated* being a music teacher.

I started to dream of something else. Anything else. I dreamt of a role where I didn't have to teach scales that I wasn't even entirely sure I understood. I dreamt of a job where I didn't need to perform music written by guys from the Jurassic Period. (No offense, Mozart. I am sure you were a hell of a guy.) I wasn't sure what I was dreaming of, but I knew it involved a path where I wouldn't wake up every morning and say again how much I hated my current life.

I had voiced my frustration out loud to God and all of humanity to hear, and apparently, he was listening. When you let God know (or when you let the universe know, whatever you decide to call the force that's bigger than you) that you're unhappy and are ready for a change, it is interesting how he will show up and do big things.

I found out about the Disney College Program. I wasn't a huge fan of the girl who told me about it; she wasn't particularly nice to me, but she happened to mention it in passive conversation, and she caught my attention. *Wait a minute,* I thought. *You're telling me I can take a semester off school; I can go to the most magical place on earth, and I can be a performer? You're telling me I won't have to sing Arias that make me want to bash my head against a wall? Where do I sign up?*

Clearly, it's not that easy, but I started down the path. Every step along the way, I tested The Big Man Upstairs in little ways. For example, on the day when I needed to meet with the Disney College program advisor, I pulled into the parking lot that is always full. I said, "Okay, here we go. If I find a parking spot, then it means I am supposed to take this internship."

Magically, there were *two* rockstar parking spots at the very front of the lot! I mean, there was no way was this a sign, right? It must be a coincidence. But still, something felt different.

I got out of my car and walked into the advisor's office, practicing a strut that I hoped would convince her I wasn't absolutely terrified. We chatted briefly about the program, and then she said, "I actually know one of the college program representatives! Let me see if we can get him on the phone. He's very busy so he may not answer, but we can try."

Perfect. I made another halfhearted deal with God. *If this mythical man answered the phone, it meant I was supposed to travel to the magical land of Disney.*

You guys, I can't even make this up. Before I could think all of the words to this wild proposition with God, *the man answered the phone.* I am not even convinced the phone rang once. Pretty sure my jaw was on the floor.

When the universe decides it wants you to follow a path, it will get you moving. With every deal I made with God, he would up the ante. It seems he wanted to make sure I knew He was serious.

After one trip to Austin, Texas, an audition, lots of paperwork, and a "congratulations" email, I was headed to Orlando, Florida to be a performer. For a girl who had never lived more than five hundred miles from Columbia, Missouri, this was utterly terrifying. But I reminded myself that this adventure was only four months (or so I thought), I moved into my 3-bedroom apartment with five other girls (yes, you read that correctly), and I started my journey with the Walt Disney Company.

I began to walk on a journey that would completely change me as a person. I would never be the same. You see, there was a guy. (Of course, there was a guy. There is *always* a guy or a girl, am I right?) I met him on my very first day at Disney. This man would change me, but not in a magical, fairy-dusted Prince Charming kind of way. I mean, he pretended to be my Prince Charming, but the pixie dust from Disney can make even danger seem magical.

Our friendship began innocently. We explored the parks and went on adventures, and he fed my adventurer side. He told me I was beautiful. He told me I was a catch. And, being the innocent baby bunny that I was, I believed him. He found someone he could manipulate. And he quickly began to feed on all of my insecurities and weaknesses.

I had no clue. I was totally oblivious. He was my Prince Charming, and I wanted to believe in this love story. I wanted to believe he would never lie to me, that he would always be my protector.

But then things shifted, and his romantic words took a different tone. He started saying things like, "Nobody is going to want to be with you because you're so emotional," or "You're the reason I said I would never date an only-child again. You're selfish and self-centered."

He said these things, and I listened. I believed him. He convinced me that my friends were all bad for me, and he said I needed to shut them out. So, I did.

He told me I was worthless. He told me I was a bad Christian. I believed him.

He told me I had anger issues, and that I needed help. I believed him.

(I will say, though, that I thank the Good Lord above that I listened to this criticism. I started seeing a therapist, and it was the single greatest choice I had made in months. Shout out to Julia and Cathy!)

I had no idea that he was slowly eroding the foundations of my life. They say love is blind. I sure was. After a few months, I caught him in a secret. I wasn't trying to find anything, but the truth found me. Crazy how that happens.

He had fallen asleep on the couch, and his phone kept buzzing. I didn't know if someone needed him, so I opened the text as I was waking him up to hand him his phone. That's when I discovered he had been sending dirty pictures and inappropriate texts to another girl. He had been caught, but clearly, he was not at fault. He told me I was the crazy one. I was the one with a problem. I needed to learn my lesson. He broke up with me, and he left me alone and broken.

Lies started to circulate about me among our circle of friends. He told everyone I was crazy, and they believed him. I heard the lies, and I believed them too.

The crushing blow came when I heard someone mention, "Well, you know about Kate and her dad, right? Let's just say... she has some serious issues."

You guys, there was no way anyone could so casually know the story of my dad and me. I didn't toss that information around easily. The story of Jack Garnes was sacred information that I shared only with the few who had walked through the mud with me. Very rarely, I gave it as a tiny token of confidence in someone new, as my way of showing that I trusted you, and only in an effort to clarify why I do the things I do. The story of my dad was precious to me, and my friends knew it. It was a very touchy subject, one I did not talk about easily.

Suddenly, in a room full of people, my story was out. I heard someone use that tiny trusted jewel as a weapon against my character. They took that gem, and they threw it against the wall. They let it fall to the ground, shattered along with any confidence, self-love, or strength I had left.

They said I was broken. I listened, and I believed them.

Have you ever felt completely alone? Have you ever faced down a crisis with the terrifying awareness that help is not on the way? It's awful to realize that the cavalry isn't coming. There is no Prince Charming to ride in on a noble

THE RECORDING: "I HAVE NOTHING LEFT TO GIVE"

steed to save you. There are no friends coming to pick you up off the floor, to hold you while you cry, to show up with ice cream and a Nicholas Sparks movie.

I had pushed away all of my support system. I had listened and believed every lie that was spoken about me. I took every verbal punch thrown my way, and somehow felt as though I deserved it.

Nobody texted to ask if I was okay.

Nobody was near to tell me I was worth fighting for.

In that moment, I was alone, and that level of loneliness is unfathomable. It cut deeper than any other heartache I had known.

Everything became gray. Everything felt numb. After a while, I felt nothing at all. I didn't feel joy. I didn't feel sorrow. I wasn't hungry. I wasn't happy. I didn't feel pain. I felt nothing. I was nothing. I had nothing left to give.

How had I let someone – or a group of someones – get me so low? I trusted them. I let them in. Of course, I listened to them. I believed it.

I want to take a moment here to say this: if you have felt that level of low, I am so sorry. If you've found yourself in this situation, or are in this situation currently, please show yourself some grace. There is a way out, and I will walk you through how I made my way to the other side. Don't give up yet, my sweet friend. Your story isn't over yet.

One night, I finally broke. I lay in my bed, staring at the ceiling. I hadn't eaten, but I knew I should be hungry. I wasn't even sure I had the strength to walk to the kitchen to try to eat. I called my mom, who was thirteen hundred miles away from Orlando. I whispered, "Mom, I have nothing. I have nothing to give. I am empty. I am just so empty."

My mom has always been my advocate, my biggest fan, and my best friend. I wanted her to say something to breathe life into me.

She said, "Now, you listen here, Kate Garnes. I did not raise you to give up and give in. I will fly down to Orlando if I need to, but listen to me. I don't know who this person is that I am talking to, but this is not my daughter. I need you to call me back when you are my daughter. I love you, but this isn't how I raised you to handle this."

I was alone. The cavalry wasn't coming.

That night, I cried every single tear out of my body. I ugly cried like everyone does at the end of *The Notebook*, or when Bing Bong jumps off the sled in the movie *Inside Out*. I allowed myself to feel empty. I allowed myself to grieve, to mourn the time I had lost when I had listened to the lies of this jerk. I mourned the friends I had pushed away and the boundaries I abandoned. And I vowed I would never let a single person steal my heart, and my soul. I had a choice to make. I could lay in this College Program Vista

Way apartment until I physically stopped living, or I could rise and fight back.

That night, I took my life back.

The next morning, I woke up with one goal for the day: I would find one thing that brought me Joy. I wasn't looking for ten. Not even two. Just one.

I walked into work, and I was hungry. If I was going to bring justice to the characters I was bringing to life, then I needed some sort of sustenance. I walked myself into the cast member cafeteria at Disney's Hollywood Studios, and you guys, I found a gift from the heavens above.

A choir of angels began to sing. A light shown down from God himself. I had found my joy: a double chocolate muffin with chocolate chips.

I had found it. The holy grail of joy. The sultan of sweets. The colossus of cupcakes. The Great Bran-Bino. I had found my joy. And in front of God and all Studios cast members, I said out loud, *"I choose you, chocolate muffin!"*

Let me get real right now about what sounds like a very awkward situation: I had nothing to lose. I had very few friends. I truly believed I was worthless. But that powerless girl found her strength and joy in a double chocolate muffin with chocolate chips. I found a spark of joy! Just one, but remember—one was all I needed. I had accomplished my goal.

This continued day after day. Wake up. Go to work. Light shines from heaven. Chocolate muffin deliciousness. Joy. Sleep. Rise, rinse and repeat. I began putting my life back together, one chocolate muffin at a time. Sounds ridiculous, right? It absolutely was ridiculous. But sometimes it is the ridiculous things, the absolutely absurd wonders, that save us.

My goal remained the same each day: find one thing of joy. But can I tell you what I discovered? The more I looked for that one thing, the more I found an abundance of things.

I discovered wildflowers on my way to work. A really solid cup of sweet coffee. A hug from a sweet three-year-old girl who loves Minnie Mouse. The late-night fireworks I could see from my apartment balcony. A fantastic book. A funny video on my social media newsfeed. A visit from my sweet Mom, just when I needed her most. As I began to keep track, they began to add up. Sometimes I found that I would even get mad at myself for only searching for one thing, not ten. The more I searched, the more I found.

That's how it works, isn't it?

When you set your mind to joy, you will find joy.

If you sent your mind to negativity, you will find annoyances, hate, and rude jerks.

If you set your thoughts to connection with others, you will find yourself in riveting conversation with a stranger at a bar, coffee shop, bookstore, or even in line for a burrito at Chipotle.

When you focus on achieving more, you will notice people entering your life who want to help you succeed.

If you set your mind to happiness, you will laugh more.

But it starts with you. It starts with what you set your mind to.

Nobody can do it for you. But you can do it yourself.

Get out there and find your joy. One chocolate muffin at a time.

Remix

What is something that brings you pure joy?

How often do you surround yourself with that thing - or anything - that brings you joy?

I challenge you to start a list.
Keep a log in a notebook, on the note section of your phone, or in your journal.
Write down the things that bring you true joy and happiness.

If that feels too hard or overwhelming, then
challenge yourself to write down just one.

One thing per day.

That's it.

And then watch how it grows.

CHAPTER 11

THE RECORDING: "I AM A GLADIATOR"

Gladiator, gladiator, gladiator
Picked a fight with the gods,
I am the giant slayer
Bone shaker, dominator
Freight train, wrecking ball,
I am the gladiator.

~ Zayde Wolf

~ ~ ~

If you catch me driving my sweet 2012 Mazda 3 while I am rocking to one of my "get hyped" songs, you will witness a one-woman concert that could rival Ariana Grande in energy, tonal clarity, and facial expressions. A few favorite songs make me ready to take on the world, wield my sword, strut like I mean it, build my empire. Nothing can stop me.

You get me, right? You know the kind of "hyped" I am talking about. I think we all have that one song. Or maybe it's a movie, a food, a beverage, or person who gets us ready to take on the battlefield of this world. It becomes our battle cry, our motto, our reminder of our strength and courage. When we hear it or see it, we instantly have a renewed energy and driving force. Sometimes it takes a minute for that saving grace to find us, but when it does, it's life changing.

That moment was no different for me. My battle cry showed up in the form of Kerry Washington in a pantsuit.

Things were tough. I had broken up with my longtime boyfriend of three and a half years, and he so promptly began dating his "best friend who is a girl" a month after our relationship ended. I was now twenty-eight, single, unmarried, and playing dress-up for a living. I was lost. I felt broken again, but in a different way than the season I wrote about in the last chapter, when the jerk wrecked my life. This was a different kind of empty. I had been stripped of my identity. I had lost my voice. I had lost my purpose. And I had to start over. Again.

The experts say that the most common stages of grief are denial, anger, bargaining, depression, and acceptance. My grief followed this pattern, but it looked more like this: ugly crying, eating my weight in tacos and chocolate, writing nasty letters to people who wronged me, burning said letters, online dating, deleting the online dating apps because people are nuts, back to tacos and chocolate, and ultimately... hours of binge-watching Netflix.

Just the healthiest of choices, if I do say so myself.

So, I was deep in the cycle when I stumbled upon the Shonda Rhymes classic television drama, *Scandal*. At first, I thought this was going to be some sort of *Twilight* meets

Pretty Little Liars kind of drama, but was I wrong. In the very first episode, the main character, Olivia Pope, played by the goddess Kerry Washington walks into a room and approaches one of the new possible candidates for her law firm. She was wearing a pantsuit that could make men shiver, and she wore heels that would make women swoon. And then she said, "We are gladiators in suits. What are you? Are you a gladiator?"

You guys. Even now. Still gets me going.

Do you remember the very first time you heard your hype song? Did the world stop moving for a moment while you wrapped your mind around the lyrics or music that were about to set your heart on fire? When I heard those words, my world stopped. I was wearing my batman pajama pants and a tank top, and my hair was pulled into a messy bun from lack of showering, but suddenly the dullness of my life was struck with a bolt of lightning.

I paused the tv. I stood up. I knew what to do.

Without missing a beat, I walked to my desk, I grabbed a dry erase marker, and I strode into my bathroom with a sense of purpose. In giant letters, I wrote across my bathroom mirror:

I AM A GLADIATOR.

I stood and stared at the words. Then I looked past the words to see my reflection.

I looked at little 5'1", 95-pound me in the mirror. I saw the reflection of a girl who had been through some tough stuff. She looked broken, weak, and lost.

But then, I saw a flame I hadn't seen in a very long time. In fact, I saw a flame I am not sure I'd ever seen before. I saw this powerful girl in a small frame, rising from the ashes of so many fires... destructive relationships, a verbally abusive father, the feelings of never being enough, and feeling alone.

I saw a gladiator.

Now let me say this. When you are a tiny person like me, and when you have always been reminded of how small you are, the last thing you feel like is a gladiator. But that became my battle cry.

I didn't run through the streets, and I didn't post it on social media. I didn't tell anyone at all. I don't share a bathroom with anyone, so nobody even saw the bold and heroic statement on my mirror. It could be my secret, this new identity. And I began to walk through my days repeating my power phrase: "I am a gladiator." When doubts crept into my thoughts, when I began to feel less than or low, I silenced the lies with my new recording of truth.

Lie: "I am weak and lame."
Truth: "No, I am a gladiator."

Lie: "I am never going to be anything."
Truth: "No, I am a gladiator."

Lie: "I am never going to find anyone to be with."
Truth: "I am strong enough on my own, because I am a gladiator."

Lie: "I am a disappointment."
Truth: "Nope, I am a gladiator."

Lie: "I will never be enough."
Truth: "I am already enough, because I am a gladiator."

I am not kidding when I say that those were the only four words that I allowed myself to hear in my head. Over and over and over again, I repeated my battle cry. I was not messing around. I took charge of my environment by posting photos of strength and quotes about confidence anywhere I knew my eyes would look. I changed the music I was listening to. No more sad, mopey Coldplay. I was all about butt-kicking, name-taking, empire-building Beyoncé, Bon Jovi, and Gaga.

All of the sudden, weird stuff started happening.

I started to walk taller.

I started to speak with confidence.

I pulled my shoulders back, instead of having them hunched forward.

I started setting boundaries and walking away from poisonous conversations and toxic people.

I reached out to good people with their own strength and confidence – people who would encourage and speak life into me.

One day, on an evening when I was having a particularly non-gladiator day, I went out for coffee with my sweet friend, Zac. He asked me a question that pushed me to a whole new level of gladiatordom. "Kate, what's something you have wanted to do for yourself that you haven't yet?"

I answered him immediately. "I want to box."

The look Zac gave me was priceless. "Like in a ring? With people?"

"Yep, because it's frowned upon to actually punch humans in normal life."

"Okay," he said. "Well, let's start with kickboxing."

Let it be known, I really hate working out. And I despise cardio.

But punching things? This I could get on board with.

I started to train as a warrior. I created a lifestyle of a gladiator. Every time I didn't want to go to the gym (which, let's be honest, was basically every day), I went anyway. I got out of bed, threw my hair into a ponytail, and walked to my car without letting myself think twice. I went straight to the gym, and I punched the stuffing out of a bag for thirty minutes. Every punch I threw at the gym, I attached to those four words. The constant through it all was those four words: "I am a gladiator."

When you set your mind to something, it's weird how your life shifts. Even the people around you react differently when you change the way you think. I started to take notice of the negative conversations and gossip happening around me. Women speaking horribly about other women. Friends hugging friends, then turning their back and verbally tearing that person apart as soon as they got out of earshot. Hurtful words pouring from the mouths of people who were just as broken as the person they were speaking about. Where was the joy? Where was the light? Where was the positivity? I didn't want to be a part of it anymore.

You know what I call those people who keep living in darkness, negativity and shame?

Peasants.

Now, before you all start sending me heated emails, let me clarify.

Yes, I know that in actual history, a gladiator was technically in a lower-class system than the peasants. Gladiators were technically slaves used for battle enjoyment. The word *gladiator* represented more of a champion or warrior mentality than the history of an actual gladiator. (It's okay, Karen, it's just a metaphor. It's going to be okay. I promise.)

Yeah, I said it. I went there. Because in no way, shape, or form am I saying I was better than any of those people. I had made the same mistakes they made. I had spoken the same hatred they spoke. I had torn down the beautiful women next to me because I was insecure and jealous. I had started rumors about my "friends," because I was jealous of the relationship they were in. I was a peasant.

But not anymore. I am not better than anyone, but that didn't mean I had to continue to surround myself with negativity. I walked away. I moved forward. I would rather walk through this world happy, joyful, and with one hundred less friends, than to be friends with everyone and live in a peasant-filled darkness. No thanks. I am good.

You see, I will not lower my standards because you can't raise yours. It is not my job to prove to you that you are beautiful. It's your job to know that you already are. It's not my job to make myself small because you are afraid to stand tall. I will not continue to live in darkness and pain, when I know I was made for more. And I would love your company on this journey to greatness, but I will not allow you to bring the hatred and the darkness with you.

You get to decide, but either way, I am building an empire.

I am running the race and climbing the mountain, with or without you.

I am a gladiator.

I am Kerry Washington in a pantsuit.

I am strong, tough, and smart.

I am not a bringer of hurt or destruction to those around me.

I don't want to sit in the mud anymore. I want a view from the good seats.

I am a gladiator.

You may be feeling a little convicted right now. You may be saying, "Yep. That's me. I sure am a bonified peasant." And that's okay. It really is. I hate to say it, but we all start there. Mostly because it's hard to know a different way in the world we live in. It's okay if that's where you are right now.

It's not your fault, but now, it is your problem.

You get to choose. You get to choose the life you live. You get to choose your attitude. You may not be able to choose where you live right now or what school you go to. You can't always pick your family. The actions of others have put you in your current situation. You may not be able to change all of that in the current moment. But there are things you are in charge of, and you can start with your battle cry. You can change your attitude. You can change what you're telling yourself.

What music are you listening to? Is it sad and depressing, or is it empowering and uplifting?

What shows or movies you are watching? Are they filled with cursing and drugs and violence, or do they make you laugh and feel encouraged?

Who are you following on Instagram, Snapchat, or twitter? Do they write all of their posts to tear others down, or is there inspiration in their words?

Think about the video games you play or the food you eat. It all matters, folks. You can change what you put in front of your face and what you put in your body. These influence you to have positive or negative thoughts, and these are things you can change.

You do have control over all of that. You have more power than you realize, my friend.

So, what is your "get hyped" reminder? Is it a prayer? Is it a quote? Is it a song or a podcast? What kind of picture is it? What does it look like? Listen to that feeling in your gut. Pay attention to what brings you power. Whatever it is, let it bring you strength. Let it remind you of your courage and remind you of your strength.

And let me be very clear, nothing that brings you clarity, joy, and positive vibes will ever be dumb or silly. This is your battle cry, not anyone else's. Find what resonates with you and be proud. You know what? Everyone else's opinion is none of your business anyway.

If you don't find yourself worthy of love, greatness and strength, nobody else will. The hard truth is nobody can give you your confidence. Nobody can do it for you. You have to make the decision to find it in yourself. But that's what a battle cry is for: to remind you of your strength when you're fighting the good fight and feel alone.

When warriors go into battle, they sound their battle cry, not only for the enemy to fear them, but to remind themselves of their bravery and strength. Failure is no longer an option for them. The same goes for you. Your life is worth living. Your story is worth telling. Your smile is worth seeing. Your light is worth shining. Failure is no longer an option for you.

Find your battle cry. Find your war chant. Yours.

What resonates with your soul? What makes your heart come alive? What makes you strut like you mean it? What makes you walk taller?

Find it. Live it. Speak it.

And watch how your life will start to change.

Remix

I want you to now search for the songs,
movies, television shows, books,
quotes—anything that motivate you.

Is there a common theme?

What is it about these things that set you on fire?

Narrow it down to three things, and then plas-
ter those things everywhere in front of you.

Write them, pin them, tweet them, post them.

Tape them to your door,

keep them in your headphones,

and speak that power into your life!

CHAPTER **12**

THE RECORDING: "YOUR OPINION IS NONE OF MY BUSINESS"

*"No, I don't want no scrub.
A scrub is a guy who can't get no love from me."*

- TLC

~ ~ ~

So, I am currently sitting on an airplane, 35,000 feet in the air, crammed against the window (my seat of choice) next to a man who has two teardrop tattoos. I am sitting here thinking about my life. How far I've come. How far I have to go. And who has joined me along the journey.

Three years have passed since I found my gladiator battle cry, and I still sound it every single day.

EVERY. SINGLE. DAY.

It's not something that I said once to myself, felt a little bit good about, and then placed on the dusty bookshelf in my room with *The Cat Who* murder mystery books and my Baby Groot bobblehead.

No, I utilize that battle cry every single day. I speak it into existence every single day.

Some days are way easier than others for me to feel like Thor and take on the world. Those are the days when I jump out of bed, eat my bagel and cream cheese like a civilized adult, put on actual pants (not sweatpants), wear a real bra, and make my way to a coffee shop to attack the world head on. I usually have music playing like Beyoncé or Journey, and I smile at everybody.

I don't mean to sound arrogant, but those are the days I kick butt. I get SO much done. Those are also the days I reach out to others, because my cup is full. I am ready to encourage the masses of anyone who will listen on their journey.

But not all days are like this.

Some days, the vortex that is my comfy bed proves to be too much for little ol' me, and I stay laying in bed. Those are the days when my battle cry isn't quite as resounding. Those are the days I tend to beat myself up for being tired or lazy. I dream about the days when I wake up with the energy to take on the world. I know I need to get up and do something. It's days like that I take out my phone... and I text my army.

Let me introduce you to my army.

These are tried and true friends who have stood the test of time. They do not let me speak negatively about myself, but they also do not let me settle. They call me out when I am making terrible life choices, or when I am making excuses for poor behavior. They are the ones who confiscate my phone when I am tempted to text an ex-boyfriend, or when I might buy a super unneeded new tank top on Amazon.

The thing is, even when they call me out, I know it's from a good place. I know it's because they love me, and they value me as a friend and as a fellow gladiator.

One of my very best friends, Missy, has been my second in command ever since my sophomore year of high school. We met in the choir room at Rock Bridge High School in 2003, and we have been inseparable ever since. She has weathered the storm of life with me for over sixteen years, and she has earned her stripes. She has loved me when I felt unlovable. She has picked me up when I couldn't move. She has celebrated my victories. She has cried with me when my heart was shattered. She has her sweet daughters call me "aunt TiTi" (they can't say Katie.. so this is the closest thing, and I wouldn't have it any other way). She earned it a spot in my very small army. She is a gladiator.

In college, I met my other very best friend, Jody. We met in sorority recruitment in 2008. It wasn't quite as instantaneous of a friendship, but serve up a few horrid breakups, the stresses of college, intramural softball, and one trip to Atchison, Kansas for a weekend of fishing and playing games, and our bond was solidified. Over ten years has passed, and she is still one of my very few go-to girls for advice, guidance, joy and sorrow. She danced with me when I found out I was working for Disney World, and I cried with her when her college sweetheart passed away unexpectedly. She earned a spot in my army. She is a gladiator.

Heidi brings in the trio of my female gladiators. She is my Disney bestie. We met when she posted on Facebook that she had a hankering for tacos, and that was it. I went to meet her, honestly thinking that more people would join us. (If I had known it was just the two of us my social anxiety would have said ABSOLUTELY NOT.) But I went, nonetheless. Four hours and several tacos later, I knew I had found someone special. It's been several years since that faithful Taco Tuesday, and this girl has never left my side. She's not afraid to be honest with me when I am doing something dumb, and she is one of my loudest cheerleaders when I succeed. I am a very lucky girl to have this trio of incredible female warriors standing behind me while I take on life.

I have to admit something, though. There have been a lot of people who have entered my life, tried to impart their wisdom or guidance, and they had not actually earned the right to give their opinion. These dangerous people HIGHLY outnumber the safe ones.

I am about to say something, and I can almost guarantee you're not going to want to hear it. So please stick with me. Ready? Here it is.

Not. Everyone. Is. Your. Friend.

THE RECORDING: "YOUR OPINION IS NONE OF MY BUSINESS"

"But Kate," you say, "you don't know my life. I have over 2,000 friends on Facebook, and I get almost 300 likes on every one of my posts."

Yep. I get it. Me too. But I am here to tell you: not everyone is your friend.

See, here's what's going to happen. You're going to start sounding your battle cry. You're going to start focusing on what you're thinking about, and you're going to begin changing your thoughts. You're going to start smiling more. You might even start laughing more. You're going to start to notice how much negative talk is around you, whether it's who you sit with at lunch, who you work with, who is on your team, or who is in your family. And it's going to become very apparent who your real friends are.

I am not talking about what I like to call "just kidding friends." You know the ones I am talking about, right? The ones who say things like, "Are you really going to wear that dress? You look like a fat pig!... I AM JUST KIDDING!!"

"You really are totally stupid, aren't you? Lights are on in your head, but nobody is home... I am just kidding!"

"You're going to turn out to be a dead beat, just like your dad, you alcoholic prick... I am just messing with you, man."

"You're never going to get a girl like Payton Sawyer. Your face looks like a pizza! She's way out of your league...I am just kidding!!"

"My God, Tiffany, did you leave any food for the rest of us to eat??? ... I am just playin' with ya', girl!"

Listen to me: These are not your friends.

THESE. ARE. NOT. YOUR. FRIENDS.

It doesn't matter if you've known them since kindergarten.

It doesn't matter if you live on the same block.

It doesn't matter if she let you borrow her sweater.

It doesn't matter if she's your sorority sister.

It doesn't matter if he's your work out partner. It doesn't matter if you share the same desk at work.

People who speak to you in this manner are not your friends.

They fall into that peasant category, remember?

You see, I am a gladiator. The more someone makes fun of me, or tells me I can't, the more they fuel my fire to prove them wrong. I don't have time to sit in the cheap seats with the peasants who spend their lives trash talking others, only to make themselves feel better.

I don't have time to let you mock or criticize me in the name of "just kidding." I want more. I dream of more. And those "just kidding friends" are not going to help me to be more or dream bigger.

One of the goals that I write down every single day is that I will have one million followers on social media. This is not because I have tricked myself into believing I will have one million friends. On the contrary.

I will have one million followers because one million people will want to follow someone who gives them encouragement, love, and strength.

I will have one million followers because I will have impacted one million people to believe they can be more than they have ever dreamed.

I will also remember that the opinions of those one million followers is none of my business. NONE. OF. MY. BUSINESS.

The opinions that are my business are the very select few people who have entered my army. I can count them on one hand. When Missy or Jody confronts me with a concern, I better stop what I am doing and listen. Why? Because they are fellow gladiators. They are striving for more in their own lives. They have stood the test of time. They would never speak unkindly to me, and they would never come to me with anything but love, even if what they are saying might be hard to hear.

When you're sounding your battle cry, and when you are living for more, those "just kidding friends" are going to rise up to try to silence you. When that doesn't work, because gladiators kneel to no human, they will leave, and you will find yourself alone.

But remember, light attracts light. Gladiators attract gladiators.

Keep pushing for more. Keep sounding your battle cry.

And I promise you, gladiators will show up. Your army will grow.

I would love to see this world taken over by gladiators of light.

But it has to start with you.

You are the only one who can take up your sword and start fighting for your own life again.

You are the only one who can change your recording from negative, self-limiting, totally lame lies, and start speaking powerful, strong, light-filled affirmations of truth.

Since I am a motivational speaker, people often ask if I just motivate myself all the time in everything.

HEAVENS NO!!! ARE YOU KIDDING ME??? I am human! I have my moments of doubt, fear, and laziness! There are plenty of days when I don't want to get out of bed, when I don't know why any self-respecting human would want to read my book, and when I wonder why anyone would listen to me speak for an hour!

But I also have my army that I lean on for truth, especially when I can't feel it. I reach out when I am feeling low or stuck. I have created a safe space for myself to be lifted back up by people who have earned their own battle scars. I don't have to do life alone, and I don't have to navigate life alone.

But to get there, I had to be SO picky. And so do you.

Be picky about your friends.

Be picky about who you date.

Be picky about the school you choose.

Be picky about the jobs you work.

Be picky about the food you eat.

Be picky about the video games you play.

Be picky about the music you listen to.

Be picky about the clothing you wear.

BE. SO. PICKY.

Listen, I get it. I get that it's not that easy to just get a new set of friends, or coworkers, or confidantes. I understand that reading this may bring up some major fear or anxiety. Please trust me, it's worth it. Those good friends are out there, but now you have to make room for them. You make room for them by getting rid of the toxicity of the peasants around you.

Life is short, folks. You don't get the time back that you've wasted on peasants and their peasant drama. You will never ever regret being picky about how you spend your time, or who you spend your time with. Time is the most valuable thing you can give anyone. Your time is important. Your time matters. So be picky on who or what you give your time to. Sound your battle cry, and remember that you and your time are worth more than any negative comment or drama.

Stand up, dust yourself off, wash your face, and start living your life as a gladiator.

The rest will fall into place.

The army will find you.

Trust yourself.

Let's rock.

Remix

How do you define a toxic friend?

Have those friends lied to you in the past?

What lies have they told you?

Who is currently in your army?

Do they deserve to be there?

If so, tell them. Thank them.

If not, get the heck out of there!

Find people who do deserve to be there!!!

It's not that easy, but it is that simple.

CHAPTER 13

THE RECORDING: "I AM WORTH FORGIVING"

"Do not let anyone enter your kingdom
unless they come with love."

- Chinese proverb

~ ~ ~

I want you to take a second and read that quote again. Read it again. Read it five more times. Do you understand the unbelievable power in that quote? Do not let anyone— ANYONE—enter your kingdom, unless they come with love.

When I read this quote, the word "kingdom" resonated with my soul. What is my kingdom?

My kingdom is my life.

My kingdom is my heart.

My kingdom is my thoughts.

My kingdom is my community.

My kingdom is this empire that I am building, to help others rise up, use their voices, and take control of their recordings back.

My kingdom is everything that I am.

So, the idea of loving my kingdom enough to stop anyone from entering unless they come with love – this is SO empowering.

Think about that. You have taken your power back. You have taken your recordings back. You have the power to stop someone from entering your kingdom unless they come with love.

Virtual high five!! Doesn't that make you feel so unbelievably powerful???

But here's the deal. As long as you're saying that nobody can enter your kingdom, unless they come with love, that includes you.

That includes the things that you say to yourself.

That includes what you think about yourself.

That includes the food you eat.

It includes the way you view yourself.

It includes the music you listen to.

It includes the TV shows you watch.

It includes all of your choices that make up every day of your life.

You see, you can stop toxic people and "just kidding friends" from speaking hate into your life every day, but it will mean nothing if you continue to speak nasty lies and hatred toward yourself in your own thoughts.

Let me ask you this. If you began to speak to your friends in the same way that you speak to yourself, would your friends stay? Would your friends hang around? Would your friends put up with it? My guess is no. No, they wouldn't stay.

Somewhere along the line, you have decided that it is totally okay for you to be your biggest critic instead of your own best advocate. Do you know what is even more dangerous? When you tear yourself down, you probably don't follow up with a "just kidding" afterwards.

When you call yourself a fat pig, you are not joking around.

When you tell yourself you are unlovable because your boyfriend or girlfriend broke up with you, you begin to truly believe you aren't worthy of love.

When you say you are the worst singer ever, you truly believe you should never belt out your favorite song in our car, because you've decided that your voice is, in fact, the worst.

When you tell yourself you are stupid because you didn't get the promotion at work or the scholarship you applied for, you believe that you are truly unintelligent and unworthy of more.

There's no "just kidding." There's no mercy. There's no room for grace.

There is only the lie, or the recording, that you're listening to, and you're believing it.

I know. I am guilty of it too.

Earlier this year, I was blessed with the opportunity to be a DJ for Walt Disney World. I didn't even realize it was something I would enjoy or be good at, but the opportunity came, and I killed it. I got to be on a microphone, celebrating everything from Disney to Dinosaurs to Villains, to No Worries. I loved my new job.

One spring afternoon, I was setting up to start the show at Disney with my coworker, Katie. Now if you've ever seen a DJ's sound board, you know that there is a big board with a lot of knobs and buttons and colorful switches that help make the music sound good. I plugged in my computer, hooked up all the wires, went to hit play... and got nothing.

Hmm. I wiggled a couple of knobs, jiggled some wires, hit play... and got nothing. Nada. No music. I calmly got my boss on the phone and explained the situation. He asked if I had my personal mixer in my car, which I did. He said to swap out the boards. I handed my phone to Katie and ran like a bat out of Hades to my car to get my board.

It took me a solid two minutes to get to my car, to get my board from my trunk, and to run back to the DJ stand. (Remember: I am not a runner. So, I was huffing and puffing all over the place. Bless my heart.) I unplugged his board as quickly as I could, set it on the seat behind me, plugged my board in, hit play... and the beautiful sound of music came through the speakers.

Nailed it. I saved the party. I did it all by myself. I am a Rockstar.

Almost.

Let's talk for a moment about how sound and motion work. See, the DJ booth was at the top of a big truck. When the music started playing, the bass started booming. When bass starts booming, things tend to bounce a little bit.

You can feel it right? Yep, I felt it. I always feel it. So did my boss's mixer board. It bounced off the seat, onto the floor, and down four stairs that led to the lower part of the truck.

Have you ever watched something happen with such magnitude that it basically unfolds in slow motion and there is absolutely nothing you can do about it? Like, when a glass of wine or soda starts to fall off a table onto white carpet, and no matter how fast you pancake dive to stop it, there is nothing you can do? The reality sets in with the gravity of what has just happened, and it truly feels like your world is crashing down around you.

That was me.

I stared at this board, now upside down at the bottom of the stairs. I stared at the little black knob that was no longer attached to the board. I stared at the slider that was now bent, and I knew for sure it could not slide anymore. I felt pretty sure in that moment that I had watched my job slip away, along with all of my dreams and my self-worth.

Mind you, this was a COMPLETE accident. It was not even remotely intentional. (Why would I do something like that intentionally?) But in my head, I was screwed. I was busted. I was in big, BIG trouble. My stomach hurt. I felt nauseous. I was either fired, or I was going to have to pay for the $1100 piece of equipment that I did not have the money to pay for.

I sent the text to my boss to tell him what had happened. He was less than happy to say the least.

I was a wreck. I finished the shift, and I went home. I called my best friend, Missy, and bawled. Y'all, I am talking the ugly cry kind of bawling.

I shared with her exactly what was happening in my head. I was a failure. I was an idiot. How could I be so stupid? Why did I ever think in a million years that I could be a DJ? Nobody else would ever make a mistake like this. I shouldn't even be a speaker, because why would anyone want to listen to someone as stupid as me? Could there be a greater failure than me? Why was she even friends with me? She deserved to be besties with someone who wasn't a total wackjob.

I took a giant gladiator-sized sword to my self-worth. I was hacking away at myself with my words. She waited for me to finish. She met me with kindness and love.

I told her, "Missy, I have to put the sword down."

"What?" she asked, confused.

"I have to put the sword down," I said. "I am a gladiator. Gladiators don't use their swords on themselves. They use their swords for truth and protection. I have to put the sword down."

Do you want to know the craziest thing of it all? My boss never said another word to me about it. He knew accidents happen, and he also knew he had insurance to cover the damage to the board. He didn't berate me, scold me, or fire me. He didn't say a single word about it.

Now, mind you, my boss is not one for confrontation, but he could have easily ended my DJ experience. And he didn't. I spent hours and hours slicing myself with my own words, dreading the job-ending phone call that never came. I worried myself sick about a scolding that was never spoken.

I made a mistake. We all make mistakes. But we don't get to take those hateful words and turn that gladiator sword on ourselves any longer.

Let's take a moment to digest that nugget of truth. How often do we do this to ourselves? We do something that feels like a failure, and it feels like we have truly messed up. We really bombed it this time. Guess what? You and me? We are human.

You are going to mess up, but that doesn't mean that you are a mistake

You are going to fail, but that doesn't mean that you are a failure.

You are a gladiator. Gladiators never use their swords on themselves. So, neither do you.

You don't get to use that sword on yourself. You don't get to speak hatred to yourself anymore. You don't get to tear yourself down and beat yourself into a tiny corner.

Now is the time to show yourself grace.

Now is when you allow yourself to be human.

You realize that it is okay to mess up. It's okay to fall sometimes, but you don't get to beat yourself up anymore. You do not allow yourself to live in that darkness. This is when you sound your battle cry.

I am going to be really honest with you: conquering your own recordings and that bully inside your head is going to be far more difficult than any toxic friendship or family member. This is because there isn't anyone you can turn to for validation. There isn't anyone to be your cheerleader in your own head. If you don't choose to disagree with the bully in your head, then the bully wins the truth.

Love yourself enough to stand up to the bully in your thoughts. Accept your power and choose to love yourself, even with the flaws and the failures. This may be the hardest thing you've ever done, but it will be the one thing that makes the biggest difference.

It's not that easy, but it is that simple.

Rise up, gladiator. We have work to do :)

Remix

Can you recall a time when you were feeling totally down on yourself for something you did poorly or failed to do at all?

How did you react?

What were the lies you told yourself?

If that same situation happened today,

could you keep from turning the nasty self-talk sword on yourself?

How could you instead handle the situation with grace and kindness?

CHAPTER 14

THE RECORDING: "I CAN SPEAK UP"

"And all those things I didn't say
Wrecking balls inside my brain
I will scream them loud tonight
Can you hear my voice this time?"

- "Fight Song" by Rachel Platten

~ ~ ~

This is a recording that I couldn't hear until fairly recently. It's one I am learning to recognize.

I spent so many years of my life feeling unworthy, misunderstood, and small. I was always taught to obey authority, so I didn't talk back, and I didn't make waves. I spent my life trying to fit into what everyone told me I needed to be. I was one of the only members of my family to professionally enter into the performing arts, so I always felt like a bit of an outsider. I didn't question decisions of my teachers or my managers at work, even when things seemed strange. I was a tiny person, with a tiny voice, taking up a tiny piece of this earth. Why would anybody listen to me?

It took a long time before I became brave enough in my own self-worth to stand up and say something when things don't seem right. I needed all the breakups, the kickboxing, and hitting rock bottom before I could climb my way up to emotional freedom. It was then that I started to become keenly aware of bullying or hatred at my workplace and in the circles I ran with.

I do believe that everything happens for a reason. And even if it doesn't, we can use whatever lesson we learn – or situation we find ourselves in – for good. However, that awareness only came as I learned my worth and my value. I had to believe I was enough just as I am in order to weather the punches of anger and hatred thrown at me.

In early January of 2017, I was chosen to open a new offering at a venue where I had been performing for a while. It was a high honor to be chosen, I got to work with a dozen of my close friends, and right next to me were some of the most incredible performers with whom I have had the honor of taking the stage. It was magical, to say the least. We were ready to bring dreams and magic to life in a way that hadn't been done before.

As the rehearsal process was wrapping up, our managers asked to do a few things that were very unsafe for an untrained performer, and none of us seasoned veterans were particularly comfortable doing it. I sat back and listened, because—remember—I don't question authority. But as the night went on, my fellow performers were quietly talking more and more about how we were not comfortable completing the task.

At 4:45 am, it was my turn to have a go at performing, and I decided to say something. I decided I would stand up for the people who may not be brave enough to stand up for themselves, and I would show just how unsafe this was. I had never questioned those above me, I had never talked back to anyone at all, so this was a big move. I made my point.

Shortly after my performance, the managers called all of my fellow coworkers and me to the front of the stage. Our managers tried to politely say, "We hear your concerns, and it's our call, not yours."

I raised my hand to calmly reply, "While we respect that you know what you are doing, we do not feel safe."

They said, "While we hear what you are saying, what we just watched happen was rude."

Now, please keep in mind, it is never my intention to upset anyone or to make anyone feel uncomfortable.

And then, a person whom we shall call *Sarah* stepped forward, stuck her finger in my face, and accused me of being the worst human alive. I was speechless.

I endured a five-minute reprimand unlike anything I had heard before. She told me that if this had been anywhere else, I wouldn't have a job anymore. She said nobody who values themselves as a professional would behave the way

I had. And she said, if she had had her way, I would never work in this city again. She said I had branded myself as a performer, so congratulations.

I was mortified. In trying to stand up for those who couldn't stand up for themselves, I had taken the brunt of some of the most hateful words ever said in my direction. And she had torn me apart in front of the entire cast. I felt like I had been punched in the gut, and like they had pulled out my gut and threw it into the moat. I started to regret my decision of speaking up.

Speaking up for those who can't is not always easy. It doesn't come with a Nobel Peace prize, and you don't get a giant sticker that reads "Great Job, Superhero." Sometimes it feels awful to do what is right or to stick up for those in need.

You get ridiculed. You get blacklisted. You lose people who have been close to you for years, because they suddenly don't want to be associated with you. And it hurts. It makes you question why you said anything in the first place. It's so much easier to stay in a place that's comfortable and to turn a blind eye and a deaf ear to those in need.

I drove home that morning in tears. I had apologized to everyone I could find. What was interesting though, was that my apologies were met with confusion. Why was I apologizing for standing up for what was right? Why was I sorry for trying to help those who wouldn't know better?

Why was I feeling shame for being brave enough to say what everyone else wouldn't? They told me that Sarah and our leaders should have been the ones apologizing for handling the situation in a completely inappropriate way.

I'll be honest I never worked at that stage again. This was a stage I had called home for many years, and because of one very short rehearsal run, I never set foot there after that. I was heartbroken at first, until I started to realize that I am enough just as I am. I know that I am a good person. I know that I am a loving and kind person. I know that I have lived a life I am proud of, which included standing up for something that was not right or safe.

Was I sad to lose something I had once loved dearly? Absolutely. I was heartbroken. Nobody ever wants to lose something that they love. But I learned something. I learned that sometimes standing up for what is right is worth losing something that is important. I could have sat back, said nothing, and let the show go on as planned., but I used my voice.

For the first time, I had a voice—and I used that voice to stand up for what I knew in my gut was right. No, it didn't end with a parade in my honor, and nobody baked a cake with my name on it. Sometimes standing up for what is right means you lose people from your life. You lose jobs or friends.

But let me ask you this, when all is said and done, and you know you did the right thing... was that job really one you wanted in the first place? Were those people truly your friends, or was that someone who needed to get the heck out of your life a while ago?

My recording used to tell me to "Stay silent."

Now my recording tells me to "Speak up."

Sometimes people may not listen, but I would rather go to bed knowing that I was brave enough to say something that nobody heard, than to watch someone get hurt or bullied, knowing I could have stopped it.

You have the choice to make. You also have a voice—a voice that the world needs to hear. You have more courage and bravery than you think. Sometimes, being brave means standing even when your knees shake, or speaking up even when your voice trembles.

Be brave, my friend. The world is counting on you.

Remix

Can you think of a time when you knew in your gut that you should speak up, but you didn't?

If you could go back, what would you do differently?

CHAPTER 15

THE RECORDING: "I HAVE A STORY WORTH HEARING"

*"Make believe I'm everywhere
Given in the light
Written on the pages
Is the answer to a never ending story"*

- *"Never Ending Story" by Limahl*

~ ~ ~

You're almost finished with this book, and let's be honest: you have a choice now.

You can think, "Okay Kate, that was great for you, but you don't know *my* life. You don't know how hard it is for me. I grew up in a broken household, I don't even have any friends, and my life is spinning out of control. I don't like my life, and I don't even like me."

The truth is, you're right. I don't know you personally.

I don't know what battles you have fought.

I don't know how hard your childhood is or was.

I don't know how many nights you have cried yourself to sleep because you felt like you just weren't enough.

I don't know how many times you have avoided looking in the mirror for fear of what you might see.

Here is what I do know:

I know that you are human.

I know that you have a soul worth loving.

I know you have a story worth hearing.

I know that winning the battle of your thoughts is going to be a very hard hurdle to jump.

I also know that it is so worth it.

I know this because I lived it. I was there. I was at rock bottom. I had found the end of my rope. I had a choice to make, and so do you.

Here's a hard truth. You may never get an apology from the person who made that ugly comment to you. You may never hear your "friend" Brittney say she was sorry for calling you stupid. You may never hear Coach Devine say you weren't a disappointment, and that you made the team proud. You may never hear your sister say you actually have a good singing voice, and she's sorry she made fun of you. You may never hear them say that it was their own insecurity that caused them to say those nasty things to you. You will probably never hear those words.

I didn't.

My dad died of alcoholism when I was twelve years old. I don't even remember if I kissed my dad goodbye the last time I saw him. I don't remember if I was even sad that he left that Christmas. I never heard him say he was truly proud of me. I never heard him say "I love you" without criticism afterwards. I never heard him say he was sorry. I lived for years with the guilt of a little girl who had always felt she was never enough. That little girl felt she couldn't get her dad to stay. She wasn't reason enough to stay, and maybe she wasn't reason enough for him to keep living. That was the guilt I carried with me for decades. I never knew there was life past those recordings my dad had given me.

The truth is, I was angry. I was angry for a long time.

Why didn't I get to be the girl whose dad takes her on daddy-daughter dates?

Why didn't I have a dad who showed me how I am supposed to be loved?

Why did I have to have the dad who was emotionally absent the entire time?

What did I do to deserve "daddy issues"?

Why didn't he show up for me?

I was sad. I was abandoned, and I was angry

The truth is, before I walked this journey, I never thought I had a story. Why would anyone want to listen to me? I was nothing special. I had no special advice or wisdom to share with anyone. I was just like everyone else: Ordinary. Unoriginal. Average.

That couldn't be farther from the truth, for me and for you.

I realized that my dad gave me a story. My dad gave me a story of learning how to overcome lies I had believed for so many years. My father left me with a story of overcoming loss and abandonment to finding hope. My dad's life story did not have a happy ending, but I now had a story to help other people learn from his mistakes and mine. I could use what those recordings – the ones I had listened to for years – to help others realize that they could be more than their own recordings.

My dad gave me a story. That story is a gift. It's a gift I am now giving to you.

Those recordings in your head, they are not your fault, my sweet friend. But they are now your problem. It's your problem if you continue listening to and living by the negative lies that you've listened to for so long. It's your problem if you continue to allow them to dictate your greatness and your potential.

But it starts with you. And it starts right now.

You have to tap faster.

Now, unless you reach out to me via social media, email, carrier pigeon, owl mail, or smoke signals, I will never know the impact of my story on your life. I will continue to speak, I will continue to write, and I will continue to live out my own truth as I build my empire.

But if just one person hears my story and starts to tap faster and make a change... then you give purpose to my dad's life. You give purpose to my life. And THAT is what it means to be a gladiator.

My friend, your story isn't over.

Your current recordings are not your permanent recordings.

It has to start with you, and it can start right now.

Find what resonates with your soul, and lean into that.

Pick your battle cry and scream it out!

Get so picky about your army, choose carefully those who earn the right to give their opinion.

Take a deep breath, wash your face, pick up your sword, and start living life as a gladiator.

Your life and your truth have been waiting.

I am not settling anymore from the view of the cheap seats.

I'll race you to the top, and we can celebrate as fellow gladiators on the mountaintop.

Whaddya say?

I am so proud of you, my sweet friend. You made it to the end of this book, and the best is yet to come.

I'll be honest, writing my journey wasn't easy. I had to face a lot of demons and truths about myself that I weren't exactly fun to dig up and relive. But it was worth it. Every single second was worth it. Sharing my journey is worth every second, if it means someone finds comfort and courage in the fact that they are not alone. They aren't the only ones who have been listening to a terrible recording for too long.

The power is now in your hands. The choice is yours. You can absolutely continue listening to the recordings you've had. You can continue to believe the limiting lies you've been listening to. But if you're feeling that small flicker of a light, listen to it. If you're seeing that tiny hope that maybe there is more to this life than the darkness you've felt, I promise... you're right.

You are the only one who can make that choice to lean in. You are worth changing the station for. You are worth finding a better way. You are worthy of leaning into that little twinkle light of hope.

You are enough.

You always have been.

So please, come, sit at my table. There is room for you here. Listen to my music, or even better, share yours with me. I am all ears.

You can do this, Gladiator.

Remix

Keep this book by your bedside, or
take it with you where you go.

When you feel that negative playlist starting again in your mind,

whip out this book. Use it as your tool-
box to override that negative playlist.

Listen to the jam that builds you up!

KATE'S GLADIATOR PLAYLIST

SIDE A

"Gladiator"
Zayde Wolf

"Survivor"
Destiny's Child

"Fighter"
Christina Aguilera

"Lost Yourself"
Eminem

"St. Elmo's Fire"
John Parr

"Fight Song"
Rachel Platten

"Stronger"
Britney Spears

SIDE B

"Run The World"
Beyoncé

"Sing"
My Chemical Romance

"Livin' On A Prayer"
Bon Jovi

"Me Too"
Meghan Trainor

"The Champion"
Carrie Underwood (Feat.
Ludacris)

"Let's Go"
Twista, Big D & Trick Daddy

"Good as Hell"
Lizzo

"Thunder"
Imagine Dragons

"Can't Hold Us"
Macklemore & Ryan Lewis

"Rise"
Katy Perry

"Born This Way"
Lady Gaga

"What's Up Danger"
Blackway & Black Caviar

"This One's for The Girls"
Martina McBride

"Here I Go Again"
White Snake

"Standing Outside the Fire"
Garth Brooks

ACKNOWLEDGEMENTS

I've never written a thank you section before, except maybe as a bio for a community theater musical. I will try to take this more seriously than thanking my cat and my unsweetened iced tea for never letting me down.

I must begin by first saying thank you, humbly on my knees, to the Lord above. You, Father, have given me a story and a drive that couldn't come from anywhere else. Thank you.

To my unbelievably supportive mom, words can't express how grateful I am to have you as my best friend, my mentor, my supporter and my champion. You have shown me the true definition of drive and love. I hope I've made you proud.

To my family, we all know that our family isn't normal, in a very good way. I love each and every one of you. I am so grateful for the guidance, prayers, laugher, hand and foot matches, vacations, and text conversations that have made our family into what it is

Grandpa Charlie, I stand in awe of the legacy you left behind. If I am one ounce of the person that you were, I've done something right.

To the insanely wise Tricia, your mentorship and counsel have pushed me to places I never dreamed I could go. Thank you for your wisdom and guidance on my journey.

Rob Lott, you were the first person to step up and start me on my journey not only of speaking, but of writing. I am always amazed at your outlook on life, and I strive to be even one tiny part of the performer that you are. Thank you for being you.

To Smack, thank you for teaching me to tap faster. You have tapped this journey with me, and I will always be grateful for the tough love, the unconditional hugs, and the doxology we would sing together.

My Missy, my soul sister, and soul mate. Thank you for loving me at my lowest, and for cheering me on at my highest. You are my ride or die, The Collin to my Mary, the Betty to Judy. I adore you always. Thank you. And to my sweet Annabelle and Lucy, I hope I can live a life that makes you proud to call me your aunt titi.

My Jody, my life changed forever when you entered it. You are the Monica to my Rachel. Thank you so much for all of your wisdom and advice you've shared as we have navigated the waters of life. After this book is published, I'm going to be in serious need of a pizza and puzzles night.

My Heidi, I'm so glad you posted on Facebook so many years ago, asking if anyone wanted to get tacos. You have guided my life in ways that you don't even know, and I am so honored to have you as my friend. Love you always.

Casey, thank you for being exactly who you are. Thank you for dealing with me waking up and typing as different stories came into my head, and thank you for holding down the fort while I'm traveling. The Sun and Stars, 5000. No stunt double. No green screen :)

To the most wonderful speaking coach, Harriet. I owe my entire speaking career – and everything I know – to you. Your wisdom and encouragement have been everything I needed.

To my Disney Family, I love each and every one of you. You all have guided my journey and truly walked this entire road of speaking and writing with me. Thank you for the laughter, the dancing, the magic, and the memories. I know we get tired, stressed, and hungry, but keep fighting the good fight. And don't be afraid to be exactly who you are. Take the dream with you, wherever you may go. I'll see you at Fant.

My 9Round family, thank you for pushing me, one round at a time. Let's go!!

Lacey Phillips, thank you for challenging me on September 10, 2016. Thank you for asking the question that changed my life.

To you, dear reader, thank you so much for reading my story. Thank you for walking this journey with me. You are the reason that I do what I do, every single day. Thank you for your love and support. I'm glad you're at my table.

And finally, to everyone who told me I couldn't do it, to those who hurt me in unspeakable ways, to every person I've cried tears over from pain, to everyone who has lied and broken my heart: thank. you. so. much. Truly, thank you. Without you, I wouldn't have the stories or the depth that I have. Because of you... I am in changing the world.

One gladiator at a time.